coloryourselfsmart
Birds of North America

The fun, visual way to teach yourself about anything and everything

By Dominic Couzens
Illustrations by David Nurney

THUNDER BAY
P·R·E·S·S

San Diego, California

Design by Shawn Dahl, dahlimama inc

Thunder Bay Press
An imprint of the Baker & Taylor Publishing Group
10350 Barnes Canyon Road, San Diego, CA 92121
www.thunderbaybooks.com

ISBN-13: 978-1-60710-218-2
ISBN-10: 1-60710-218-8

Printed in China
1 2 3 4 5 15 14 13 12 11

CONTENTS

INTRODUCTION

BIRDS ARE AMONG THE MOST COLORFUL AND VISIBLE OF ALL LIVING CREATURES. It is fitting, therefore, to let their colors and plumage patterns teach us about their lifestyles. In this book, you will get to know some North American birds by coloring in snapshots of their plumage and other physical characteristics, and discover how these affect bird behavior and ecology.

In the United States, we have about 750 breeding or regularly visiting species of birds, ranging from familiar backyard neighbors such as Blue Jays and Chickadees to much rarer and more exotic characters such as the Magnificent Frigatebird and the Bohemian Waxwing. Every one of these species has a story to tell, but for the purposes of this book we have selected just 52. They have been chosen for a number of reasons. Some are everyday birds, whose lifestyles demand a closer look. Others are widespread species that are representative of some kind of lifestyle or behavior, and still others are less common, yet exhibit extremes of plumage and deed that make them irresistible subjects to depict. Thus, we have included such superb birds as the Greater Sage-Grouse, the Black Skimmer, and the Acorn Woodpecker, each of which is spectacular in how it looks and in what it does.

Each of the species included has a portrait for you to color in and ten labels telling you things that you can see, or sometimes infer, from the illustration. Each species also has a brief introduction on the facing page, and by drawing together all these threads, you will gain a few insights into what makes each bird different from the rest, and why it is interesting or unusual. In some cases, the main portrait depicts a specific behavior associated with the bird. And where additional points need to be made, about half of the birds include more detailed images, including close-ups of unique body parts. And just for fun, a few species have a fact box containing a piece of information that will hopefully amaze you.

Happily, the birds on our continent can be found more or less everywhere: from the ocean to inland waterways, from the ground to high in the sky, from dense forests to prairie, and from the wildest places to city centers. The birds in this book are grouped into different sections, where birds are related in some way or another, be it their habitat, relationships, or behavior. In this way we hope to present the birds in a way that is easy to understand and appreciate.

All birds are covered with feathers, of course. Birders and scientists have names for all the feather tracts, and often the individual feathers themselves. It is useful for the enthusiast to know a few of these names, but on the whole we have avoided including too much technical information. A couple of species, such as the Western Kingbird and Bar-tailed Godwit, include some of the appropriate labels.

The idea of this book, then, is to color in and learn about the birds in a fun way. And once you have colored in all 52 plates, try the quiz at the end, which you might well find quite challenging. Overall, we do hope that this book enhances your enjoyment of the birds, both in your backyard and further afield.

ABOUT THE COLOR YOURSELF SMART SERIES

COLOR YOURSELF SMART is a revolutionary new series designed to help improve your memory and make learning easy. Leading memory and learning experts agree that color and illustrations help to reinforce difficult subject matter and greatly increase your chances of both creating visual memories and recalling that information faster. So if you find it difficult to remember something—even after you've just read it—then it's time to start coloring your way to faster learning and a sharper memory!

Color Yourself Smart: Human Anatomy
Color Yourself Smart: Geography
Color Yourself Smart: Birds of North America

HOW TO USE THIS BOOK

A pack of eight artists' studio-quality coloring pencils from Faber-Castell are included with this book, however, you should feel free to supplement these colors with your own as you see fit—the more colors you have available to you, the more enjoyable you will find memorizing the material. A colored plate section is included at the back of the book, showing all of the featured illustrations colored in for your reference, and a color key accompanies those illustrations that are more complicated in nature, for readers who prefer a little more guidance.

Keep your pencil tips pointed with the accompanying sharpener and use the eraser to correct any mishaps. The eraser is more effective when used on lighter washes of color and may not be so helpful if you have pressed too hard with one of the darker colors.

COLORED PENCIL TECHNIQUES

Numerous finishes can be achieved with colored pencils, depending on how they are used. Artists' quality pencils can be smudged for a watercolor effect and different colors can be blended to create other colors. When blending pencil colors, it is best to lay down the lighter colors first and overlay the darker colors to achieve the desired effect.

Pressing harder or lighter on the paper will also give a different shade of color. It is easier to use the side of a pencil point to wash large areas with color, and use a sharp point for those areas that require more careful coloring or more detail.

Western Grebe | *Aechmophorus occidentalis*

Breeds locally in the West from Alberta and Saskatchewan south to California, Arizona, and New Mexico, with an eastward extension to Minnesota and Wisconsin. Winters mainly on the Pacific coast.

WITH ITS UNREMARKABLE BLACK-AND-WHITE PLUMAGE and relatively restricted distribution, the Western Grebe would probably never have attracted much attention among birders except for one thing: its extraordinarily elaborate and graceful courtship routines. The grebes in this illustration are caught up in the middle of the so-called "Rushing Display," in which two birds rear up on the water and run across the water surface, sometimes for distances as long as 65 feet (20 m). Although this display is the most famous, there are many others, too. In another ceremony, two grebes present pieces of weed to each other, and in others, the birds bob their heads and "pretend" to preen.

Grebes are among the most aquatic of all birds. Their feet are set so far back on their bodies that they are almost incapable of moving on land. But when it comes to swimming, they can attain speeds underwater in excess of over 3 feet (1 m) per second, using powerful strokes of their lobed feet. Owing to the almost complete absence of a tail, these feet can be rotated freely in the back, giving supreme maneuverability and control.

Western Grebes breed in colonies, mainly on inland freshwater lakes with a combination of extensive open water (usually several square miles) and rich vegetation on the margins. In the winter, they almost all migrate to the coast.

DID YOU KNOW?

Intriguingly, although it is most typical for a male and a female to perform this rush, sometimes a male will enlist another male to ballet across the surface, simply to gain the attention of a female.

10 THINGS TO REMEMBER

1. Long, pointed bill is used for lunging at fish in the water, usually grabbing but occasionally spearing.

2. Very long neck has mechanism that thrusts head powerfully forward when grabbing for fish.

3. Greenish-yellow bill and black beneath eye distinguish Western Grebe from a very close relative, Clark's Grebe (orange-yellow bill).

4. Brilliant red eyes. The intense color of the eyes is due to the constricted pupil, an adaptation to viewing in low light levels underwater.

5. Short wings allow grebes to fly, but not powerfully.

6. In display, main flight feathers are folded, and only the inside feathers—the scapulars—are opened.

7. Feet set at the back of the body paddle with greater vigor to keep displaying bird upright.

8. Birds rush parallel to one another in display.

9. The kink of the neck is unique to this display.

10. Feet are lobed, not webbed, to give the grebe great flexibility and control.

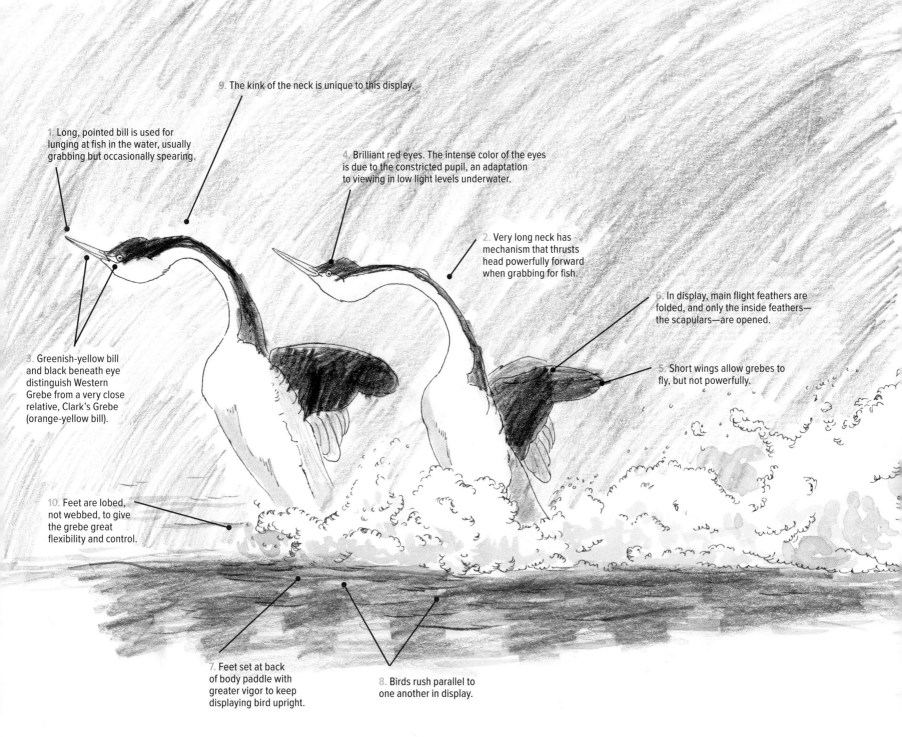

9. The kink of the neck is unique to this display.

1. Long, pointed bill is used for lunging at fish in the water, usually grabbing but occasionally spearing.

4. Brilliant red eyes. The intense color of the eyes is due to the constricted pupil, an adaptation to viewing in low light levels underwater.

2. Very long neck has mechanism that thrusts head powerfully forward when grabbing for fish.

6. In display, main flight feathers are folded, and only the inside feathers—the scapulars—are opened.

3. Greenish-yellow bill and black beneath eye distinguish Western Grebe from a very close relative, Clark's Grebe (orange-yellow bill).

5. Short wings allow grebes to fly, but not powerfully.

10. Feet are lobed, not webbed, to give the grebe great flexibility and control.

7. Feet set at back of body paddle with greater vigor to keep displaying bird upright.

8. Birds rush parallel to one another in display.

Brown Pelican | *Pelecanus occidentalis*

Present all year along the Pacific coast in California; on the East Coast from Maryland southward to Florida, and along the Gulf Coast to west Texas.

THIS UNMISTAKABLE, COLORFUL PELICAN is found both on the East and West Coasts, and is the only member of its family to be exclusively marine in habitat. It breeds in colonies on islands, cliffs, or mangroves, and feeds out to sea, usually inshore but occasionally much farther out.

Most pelicans feed by scooping fish into their pouches while swimming, but the Brown Pelican is unique in its habit of aerial hunting. Flying as high as 65 feet (20 m) in the air, it spots a fish and plunges down onto it, head first, grabbing the unsuspecting prey upon entry. The legs and wings are thrust back as the bird enters the water. Once the fish is ensnared, the pelican has to drain its bill of water. Remarkably, the weight of fish and water carried can exceed the weight of the bird itself.

Despite their size and weight, pelicans fly well and can soar for hours on end. This helps them to travel long distances when looking for a good place to feed.

DID YOU KNOW?

Brown Pelicans make use of their feet while incubating, balancing the eggs on the webs between their toes.

10 THINGS TO REMEMBER

1. Long bill is movable and acts as a "lid" for the pouch.

2. Unique pouch is used to scoop up fish and hold them.

3. Makes head-first plunge-dives.

4. When diving, the angle of each wing tip is constantly adjusted to home in on prey.

5. Color of bill and pouch varies geographically. The red on the pouch indicates that this is a West Coast bird. East Coast birds have dark brown pouches.

6. Long, broad wings enable pelican to save energy by soaring.

7. Webbed feet help the pelican to swim well.

8. Short legs help to carry the bird's extreme bulk on land.

9. Tip of bill is sensitive to the movement of fish in the water.

10. Crest used in display.

6. Long, broad wings enable pelican to save energy by soaring.

8. Short legs help to carry pelican's extreme bulk on land.

10. Crest used in display.

3. Makes head-first plunge-dives.

4. When diving, the angle of each wing tip is constantly adjusted to home in on prey.

1. Long bill is movable and acts as a "lid" for the pouch.

2. Unique pouch is used to scoop up fish and hold them.

9. Tip of bill is sensitive to movement of fish in the water.

5. Color of bill and pouch varies geographically. The red on the pouch indicates that this is a West Coast bird. East Coast birds have dark brown pouches.

7. Webbed feet help pelican to swim well.

Northern Pintail | *Anas acuta*

Breeds throughout Alaska and continental northern Canada east of Hudson Bay, south through the Prairie Pothole region of the Dakotas, Wisconsin, and Minnesota; also from Oregon south to California, the Great Lakes region, Labrador, and Quebec. Winters in much of the southern United States.

ELONGATED BOTH IN FRONT AND BEHIND, the Northern Pintail is an abundant duck of the northern Prairies and the Arctic, breeding in productive shallow pools, and wintering over much of the continent. It is an omnivore, feeding on both animal and plant material that it gathers from shallow water or while grazing. Pintails, with their long necks, can forage in deeper pools than, for example, a competitor such as a Mallard. In common with other ducks, the bill is flattened, and the edges of both mandibles are fitted with toothlike projections that overlap, so that matter is filtered out when water is forced through the sides of the bill by the tongue.

Male Pintails perform collective displays, during which they call and show off various parts of their striking plumage, including the tail plume. Competition for females is rife, and the males can often be seen lifting their chin to try to ward off a rival.

10 THINGS TO REMEMBER

1. (F) Female mainly has pale brown plumage for camouflage when nesting.

2. (M) Male has bright colors and pattern for display. He pays little attention to nesting.

3. (F) One of its principal feeding techniques is "up-ending," keeping upside down by kicking the feet so the bill can reach bottom ooze. The bill can reach down almost 2 feet (50 cm).

4. (M) Slim body shape allows for speed and mobility in flight.

5. (M) Long neck for reaching down to the bottom of shallow water.

6. (M) Flattened bill used for filter-feeding.

7. (M) Nail of bill is used for draining water as the bird touches surface.

8. (M) Long tail of male is an ornament used in display. It can be pointed upright.

9. (M) Prominent black-and-yellow rear end shown off in "head-up, tail-up" courtship display.

10. (M) Prominent white stripe shown off in special display to lead female away.

Main picture is male (M),
female (F) in background

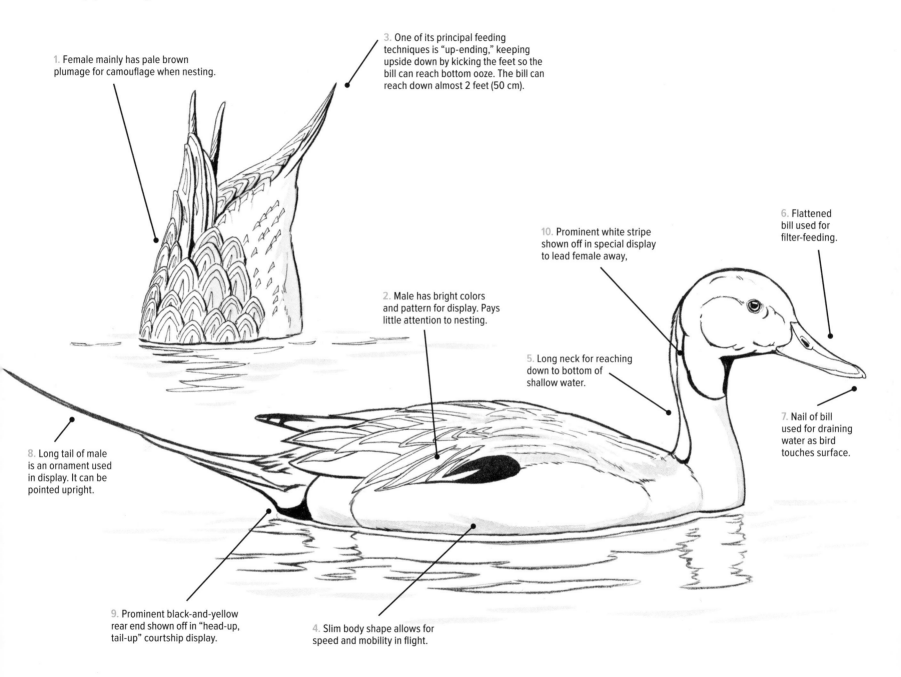

1. Female mainly has pale brown plumage for camouflage when nesting.

3. One of its principal feeding techniques is "up-ending," keeping upside down by kicking the feet so the bill can reach bottom ooze. The bill can reach down almost 2 feet (50 cm).

6. Flattened bill used for filter-feeding.

10. Prominent white stripe shown off in special display to lead female away,

2. Male has bright colors and pattern for display. Pays little attention to nesting.

5. Long neck for reaching down to bottom of shallow water.

7. Nail of bill used for draining water as bird touches surface.

8. Long tail of male is an ornament used in display. It can be pointed upright.

9. Prominent black-and-yellow rear end shown off in "head-up, tail-up" courtship display.

4. Slim body shape allows for speed and mobility in flight.

Long-tailed Duck | *Clangula hyemalis*

Breeds in Alaska and Arctic Canada, including the islands, south to Manitoba and east to Labrador. Winters down the Pacific coast to Oregon, on the Great Lakes, and down the East Coast as far as Chesapeake Bay.

FORMERLY KNOWN AS THE "OLDSQUAW," the Long-tailed Duck is a true Arctic species that breeds on tundra pools as far as 80 degrees north, where it can be very numerous and conspicuous. Besides the bold plumage, it is very noisy, making calls which have a clanging, far-carrying quality, and birds will sometimes call together, which makes them hard to miss.

In contrast to many ducks, Long-tailed Ducks form close pair-bonds which may persist for several years. On the tundra, the male usually holds a territory, while the female performs all of the breeding duties. Once the chicks have hatched, the males depart from the breeding areas.

In many ways, the Long-tailed Duck lives a double life, and this is reflected in the very distinct plumage adopted in different seasons. Quite inconspicuous and brown in summer, trying not to attract the attention of nest predators such as Arctic Foxes and gulls, the male has a much showier plumage in the winter and early spring, and it is in this plumage that he will display and court.

The birds form large flocks in winter and are found out at sea, sometimes far from land. They feed on crustaceans, mollusks, and fish, and are thought to be able to dive down deeper than any other duck in the world, possibly to depths of almost 200 feet (60 m).

10 THINGS TO REMEMBER

1. [W] Males in this plumage are seen between November and April, which includes the season when they pair up.

2. [W] Bold markings on head shown in "chin-lifting" display.

3. [W] Long, spiky tail is lifted up over back during other displays.

4. [W] Underparts are pale, which is typical for a bird that dives underwater. It means that it cannot be seen easily from below against the light.

5. [S] Males in this plumage are seen in May and June.

6. [S] Dark plumage helps to conceal bird against dark pools and vegetation on the tundra. In most duck species, males don't keep near to nest, but these long-tailed ducks do.

7. [S] Ducks of this species often have plumes over the back.

8. Streamlined body sits low in the water.

9. As befits a supreme diving duck, the feet are set far back on the body so that they can propel the bird from the back. When underwater, this species also uses its wings.

10. Small but sturdy bill enables these ducks to crush mollusks and other hard prey.

16

COLOR YOURSELF **SMART**
BIRDS OF NORTH AMERICA SWIMMING BIRDS

Male winter (W), top
Male summer (S), bottom

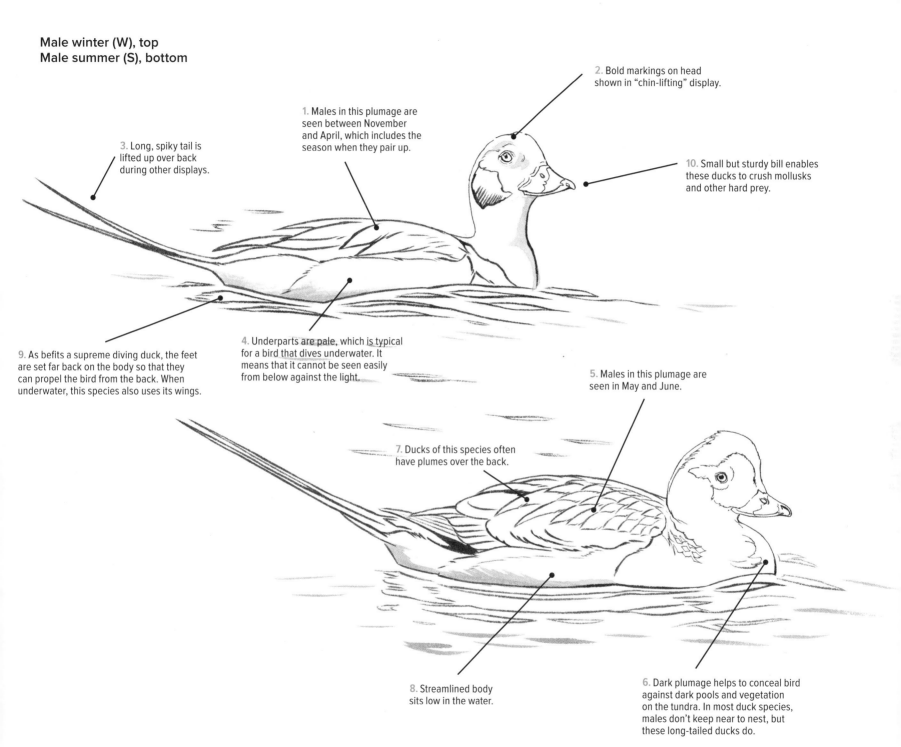

2. Bold markings on head shown in "chin-lifting" display.

1. Males in this plumage are seen between November and April, which includes the season when they pair up.

3. Long, spiky tail is lifted up over back during other displays.

10. Small but sturdy bill enables these ducks to crush mollusks and other hard prey.

9. As befits a supreme diving duck, the feet are set far back on the body so that they can propel the bird from the back. When underwater, this species also uses its wings.

4. Underparts are pale, which is typical for a bird that dives underwater. It means that it cannot be seen easily from below against the light.

5. Males in this plumage are seen in May and June.

7. Ducks of this species often have plumes over the back.

8. Streamlined body sits low in the water.

6. Dark plumage helps to conceal bird against dark pools and vegetation on the tundra. In most duck species, males don't keep near to nest, but these long-tailed ducks do.

Tufted Puffin | *Fratercula cirrhata*

Breeds along the Pacific coast from Alaska (including Aleutians) to California (rare). Winters far out in ocean.

THE MAGNIFICENT TUFTED PUFFIN occurs along the length of the Pacific coast, from northern California to Alaska, becoming generally more common the further north you go. It breeds on cliffs and offshore islands, digging its own burrow as deep as 6 feet (2 m) into soil, or simply selecting a suitable crevice among rocks for its single large egg. The egg is laid in a chamber at the end of the burrow and takes about 40 days to hatch. Once ready to leave, the young depart at night on their own, without the adults' knowledge.

During the stage that the chick is in the nest, both sexes bring fish deliveries twice a day, making four in total. They carry the fish crossways in the bill, as depicted in the illustration on the right. They don't stand on ceremony; the fish are delivered and the adult leaves in less than a minute.

The extraordinary orange bill and curved, strawlike tufts are part of the breeding dress, and they are lost in the nonbreeding season. In winter, the Tufted Puffin often swims far out to sea and is rarely seen by people.

10 THINGS TO REMEMBER

1. Dark coloration of plumage is maintained through the year.

2. Small wings are used for "flying" underwater when foraging. In air, they are beaten fast for rapid, but energy-sapping flight.

3. Bill is broad, but flattened in lateral plane. Bright colors used in many displays.

4. Bill has grooves on upper mandible for holding slippery fish.

5. Fish are held crossways in bill. Usually carries 5–20 fish, maximum 29.

6. Back set feet are ideal for swimming and walking, but they make taking off from water surfaces difficult.

7. Webbed feet act as rudders for this bird.

8. Claws allow bird to cling to surface of slippery rocks, and also to dig and burrow.

9. Pink rosettes at base of mouth are shown off to female in display.

10. Unusual strawlike plumes are lost in winter.

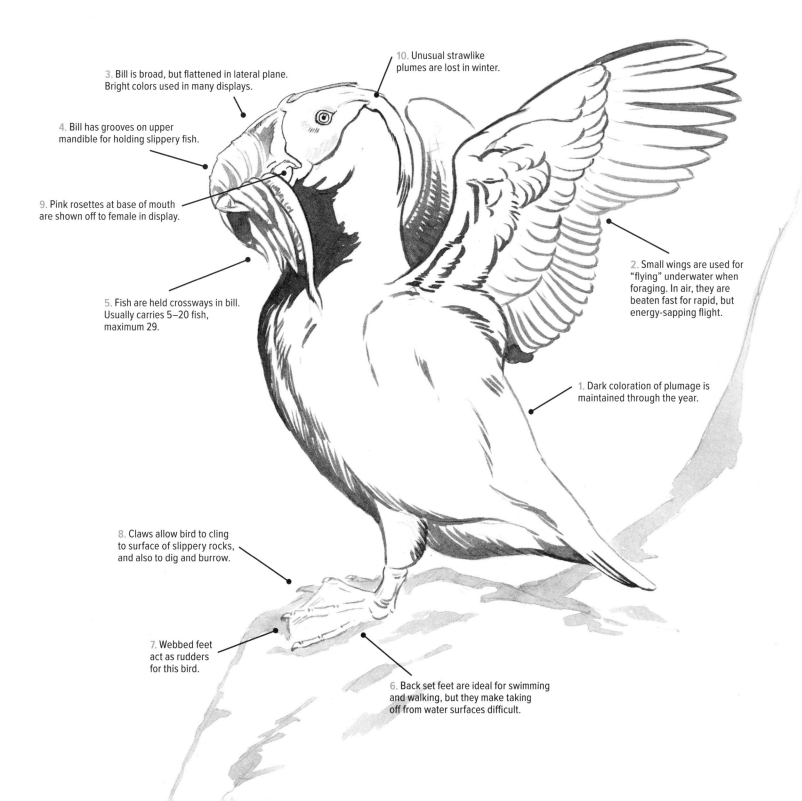

3. Bill is broad, but flattened in lateral plane. Bright colors used in many displays.

10. Unusual strawlike plumes are lost in winter.

4. Bill has grooves on upper mandible for holding slippery fish.

9. Pink rosettes at base of mouth are shown off to female in display.

5. Fish are held crossways in bill. Usually carries 5–20 fish, maximum 29.

2. Small wings are used for "flying" underwater when foraging. In air, they are beaten fast for rapid, but energy-sapping flight.

1. Dark coloration of plumage is maintained through the year.

8. Claws allow bird to cling to surface of slippery rocks, and also to dig and burrow.

7. Webbed feet act as rudders for this bird.

6. Back set feet are ideal for swimming and walking, but they make taking off from water surfaces difficult.

Magnificent Frigatebird | *Fregata magnificens*

Breeds only in Florida. Regular nonbreeding visitor to the Pacific coast of California, the Gulf of California, the Salton Sea, the Gulf of Mexico, and the East Coast as far as North Carolina.

THE MAGNIFICENT FRIGATEBIRD IS A RARE BIRD IN THE UNITED STATES, breeding only in the Dry Tortugas of Florida and visiting the nearby Gulf Coast. It also sometimes turns up as a stray on either coast, perhaps getting lost as it wanders the oceans for food.

Frigatebirds are strongly adapted for a life of flying. They hardly ever land or swim, and their feet are small and poorly webbed. The wings, however, are long and slender, the body is streamlined, and the tail is forked, all of which means that the Frigatebird can glide for hours without a flap. These birds also have, relative to their size, the lightest skeleton of any known bird, accounting for just 5 percent of their body weight—less than the feathers! The bones are partially hollow and filled with air.

Apart from snatching fish (especially flying fish) and squid from the water surface, Frigatebirds also steal from other birds, especially as the latter return to their colonies with food for the young. They do this by flying menacingly behind a victim, using their supreme agility to keep on a bird's tail until it surrenders its hard-earned catch.

Frigatebirds breed in colonies, building a flimsy nest in a bush or mangrove, usually on an island. The males display by inflating their pouch and vibrating the bill against the skin of their pouch, making a drumming sound.

10 THINGS TO REMEMBER

1. Large bird, with a wingspan of approximately 5–8 feet (1.7–2.4 m)—as much as a Bald Eagle.

2. Small feet are barely visible. The Frigatebird spends almost all its life in flight.

3. Long, forked tail for braking and changing course.

4. Long, pointed wings allow for speed, acceleration, and twisting and turning.

5. Wings are large relative to body weight (low wing-loading), which saves energy.

6. Hooked bill is used for scooping fish or other items from the water's surface.

7. Body and wing feathers aren't waterproof.

8. Dark plumage gives hawklike appearance, which helps to intimidate victims during food piracy.

9. Male has red air sac on throat. Frigatebirds are the only seabirds in which the plumage of the sex differs.

10. Air sac is inflatable, as seen here. This is used in display to the female, usually with bill clattering as accompaniment.

COLOR YOURSELF **SMART** BIRDS OF NORTH AMERICA OTHER WATER BIRDS

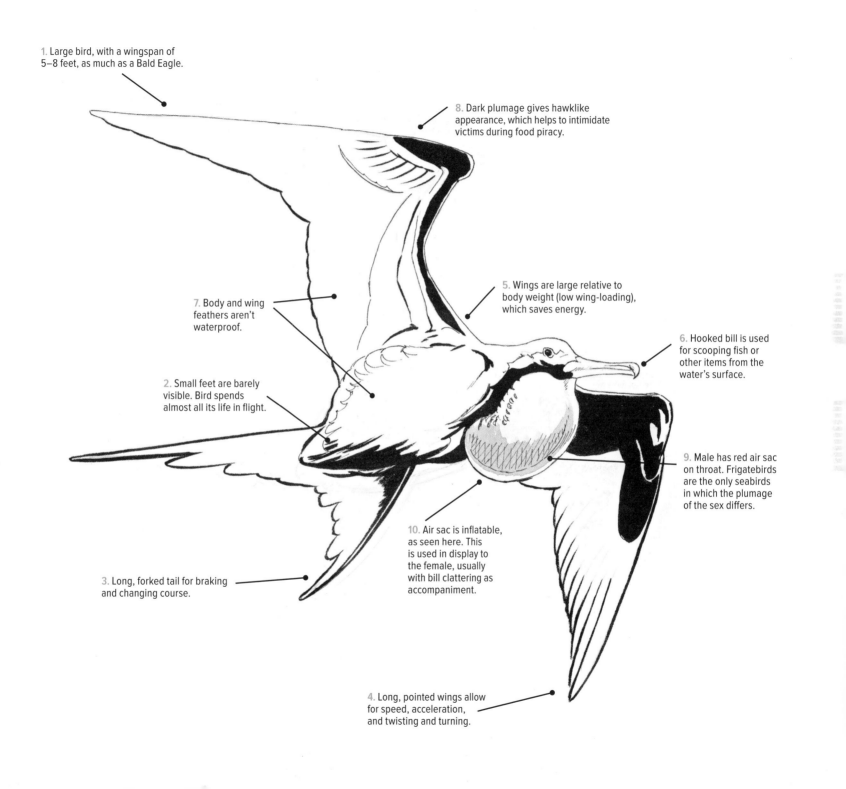

1. Large bird, with a wingspan of 5–8 feet, as much as a Bald Eagle.

8. Dark plumage gives hawklike appearance, which helps to intimidate victims during food piracy.

7. Body and wing feathers aren't waterproof.

5. Wings are large relative to body weight (low wing-loading), which saves energy.

6. Hooked bill is used for scooping fish or other items from the water's surface.

2. Small feet are barely visible. Bird spends almost all its life in flight.

9. Male has red air sac on throat. Frigatebirds are the only seabirds in which the plumage of the sex differs.

10. Air sac is inflatable, as seen here. This is used in display to the female, usually with bill clattering as accompaniment.

3. Long, forked tail for braking and changing course.

4. Long, pointed wings allow for speed, acceleration, and twisting and turning.

Ivory Gull | *Pagophila eburnea*

Breeds in Arctic Canada on only five islands: Baffin, Ellesmere, Cornwallis, Seymour, and Devon. Outside the breeding season, it can be seen regularly in the Bering and Labrador Seas, though it occasionally strays elsewhere.

ONE OF THE FEW BIRDS IN THE WORLD that has completely white plumage (at least in the adults), the Ivory Gull provides a good example of cryptic coloration. It is one of the few birds to live year-round in the northern Polar region, both in Canada and Eurasia, where it is never far from pack and drift ice.

It was once thought that Ivory Gulls were dependent upon waste and carrion for their food, but in fact their long bill, useful for making dexterous snatches from the water surface, hints at their major food source, small fish. They often feed in the dark, when small fish and squid come closer to the water surface. However, they do often attend Polar Bear kills and seal colonies, tucking into carrion without hesitation.

The Ivory Gull breeds in small, scattered colonies, both on cliffs and flatter, rockier places like gravel banks. Birds arrive at their breeding sites already paired, and the nesting cycle is compressed into a rapid 60-day period because of the short Arctic season.

10 THINGS TO REMEMBER

1. White plumage helps the Ivory Gull to blend in with its pack-ice habitat. The Ivory Gull is the only gull that is entirely white.

2. Long bill enables the bird to snatch fish from the water surface, and its bill coloration is unique among gulls.

3. The black legs are short, which cuts down on heat loss through them.

4. The feathers on the leg reach down to the tibio-tarsal joint, cutting down on heat loss.

5. The wings are long, enabling the bird to fly nimbly.

6. Large, dark eyes enable bird to feed in low light intensities, essential during the Polar winter.

7. Juvenile has quite a different bill and head pattern from the adult, which helps individual recognition and maintains the hierarchy.

8. Frequently seen feeding at carcasses on the pack-ice, as well as on feces and offal.

9. Blood on the ice beside a carcass will also be eaten by the Ivory Gull.

10. Red color (as here on carcass) acts as a strong attractant. It is also attracted to red items left by campers and explorers.

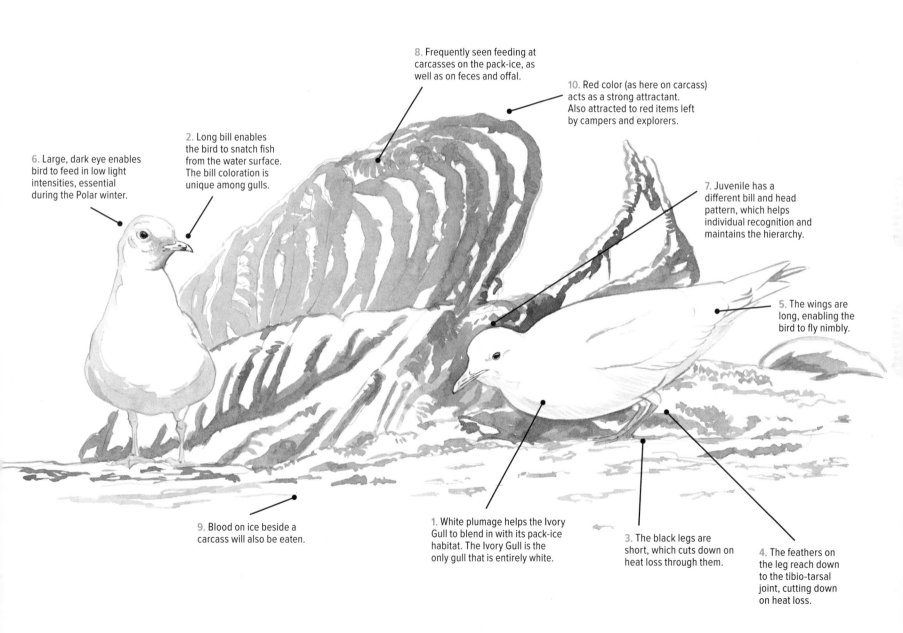

8. Frequently seen feeding at carcasses on the pack-ice, as well as on feces and offal.

10. Red color (as here on carcass) acts as a strong attractant. Also attracted to red items left by campers and explorers.

2. Long bill enables the bird to snatch fish from the water surface. The bill coloration is unique among gulls.

6. Large, dark eye enables bird to feed in low light intensities, essential during the Polar winter.

7. Juvenile has a different bill and head pattern, which helps individual recognition and maintains the hierarchy.

5. The wings are long, enabling the bird to fly nimbly.

9. Blood on ice beside a carcass will also be eaten.

1. White plumage helps the Ivory Gull to blend in with its pack-ice habitat. The Ivory Gull is the only gull that is entirely white.

3. The black legs are short, which cuts down on heat loss through them.

4. The feathers on the leg reach down to the tibio-tarsal joint, cutting down on heat loss.

Black Skimmer | *Rynchops niger*

Breeds along the East Coast from Massachusetts and Long Island right down to Florida, and along the Gulf Coast to Texas. Winters in the Carolinas southward, and also in Southern California.

THERE ARE FEW BIRDS MORE INSTANTLY RECOGNIZABLE than the Black Skimmer, a bird with a unique bill shape and method of feeding. Mainly occurring along coasts and always near shallow, calm lagoons and pools, this bird catches fish or shrimps by literally skimming over the water, flying in a straight line, allowing its long lower mandible to slice along the surface. When the bill tip touches a fish, the upper mandible slams down on to the lower, while the head and neck bow down to keep the prey in its jaws. When hunting, the Skimmer will often fly along for over 300 feet (100 m) or so, before turning back and plowing the same or a similar furrow again. And because it uses touch to locate food, it can feed in twilight, or even at night.

Black Skimmers occur mainly along the East and Gulf Coasts, where they breed in colonies, each bird making loud calls like the barking of dogs. The nest is on the ground of an open shallow sandbar or beach. The 4–5 young are fed by regurgitation; when they fledge, their bill tips are of equal length.

10 THINGS TO REMEMBER

1. Unique bill shape: upper mandible is shorter than lower.
2. [Flying bird] Tip of the lower mandible is like the blade of a knife, and slices through water.
3. Upper mandible is slightly downcurved, and it fits into the groove of the lower mandible.
4. Base of bill is broad, for swallowing fish.
5. The white plumage underneath the Skimmer makes them difficult for prey to spot from below bird.
6. The dark plumage on top of the Skimmer makes it difficult for predators to spot them from above.
7. Large eyes for seeing in the dark. The eyes often "disappear" in the black cap plumage, which also reduces glare.
8. Long wings for efficient, buoyant flight.
9. Webbed feet play a part in losing heat. The Skimmer will sometimes drag feet and breast feathers through water for cooling.
10. Very sociable birds. Flying flocks often coordinate their maneuvers.

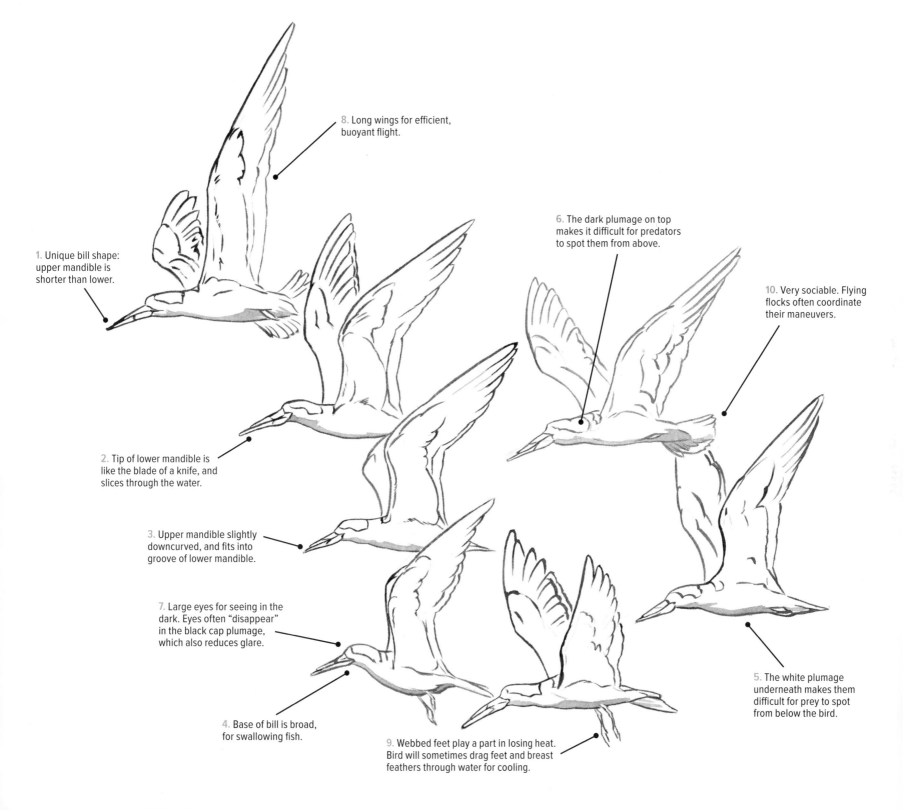

8. Long wings for efficient, buoyant flight.

6. The dark plumage on top makes it difficult for predators to spot them from above.

10. Very sociable. Flying flocks often coordinate their maneuvers.

1. Unique bill shape: upper mandible is shorter than lower.

2. Tip of lower mandible is like the blade of a knife, and slices through the water.

3. Upper mandible slightly downcurved, and fits into groove of lower mandible.

7. Large eyes for seeing in the dark. Eyes often "disappear" in the black cap plumage, which also reduces glare.

4. Base of bill is broad, for swallowing fish.

9. Webbed feet play a part in losing heat. Bird will sometimes drag feet and breast feathers through water for cooling.

5. The white plumage underneath makes them difficult for prey to spot from below the bird.

Reddish Egret | *Egretta rufescens*

Present all year in parts of Florida and the Gulf Coast.

NO OTHER LARGE WADING BIRD IN NORTH AMERICA utilizes as many active methods of catching food as the Reddish Egret. Aside from the usual wading in water, typical of herons, it will also physically disturb fish by half-running, half-jumping, flicking its wings in and out, and jabbing right and left; if this doesn't work, it will open its wings to make a canopy, luring fish into its self-made shade; or it will sometimes paddle its foot in the water to disturb food this way. Occasionally it has even been seen hovering over the water and then lunging.

You might think that such a diversity of feeding techniques might make the Reddish Egret successful, but it is in fact the rarest of our herons, being found chiefly in Florida and the Gulf Coast. The total population is only about 2,000 pairs. It is exclusively coastal in habitat and usually nests in mangrove swamps.

Curiously, the Reddish Egret is found in two color forms, reddish and white. Pairs are often mixed.

10 THINGS TO REMEMBER

1. Long legs for wading in water depths of about 10 inches (25 cm).

2. Daggerlike bill for lunging at fish.

3. Plumes on back of head are used in display, the head and neck being stretched up. These plumes were once harvested by people for fashionable hats.

4. Long neck for watching the water from above. Herons have special vertebrae that "snap" forward, increasing the speed of the lunge.

5. Often flicks wings open to disturb fish, which it then catches.

6. Broad wings create shade, and fish are thought sometimes to take "refuge" under an Egret's canopy.

7. Comes in two color forms, or morphs. The other morph is pure white.

8. The two-toned bill is found in adult breeding birds only; in the nonbreeding season, the bill is all dark.

9. Forward-set eyes help to judge distance (the fields of the two eyes overlap, hence objects can be seen from two different angles).

10. Tail is short to keep out of the water.

5. Often flicks wings open to disturb fish, which it then catches.

6. Broad wings create shade, and fish are thought sometimes to take "refuge" under birds' canopy.

3. Plumes on back of head are used in display, the head and neck being stretched up. The plumes were once harvested by people for fashionable hats.

9. Forward-set eyes help to judge distance (fields of the two eyes overlap, hence objects can be seen from two different angles).

7. Comes in two color forms, or morphs. The other morph is pure white.

2. Daggerlike bill for lunging at fish.

10. Tail is short to keep out of water.

8. The two-toned bill is found in adult breeding birds only; in the nonbreeding season, it is all dark.

4. Long neck for watching the water from above. Herons have special vertebrae that "snap" forward, increasing the speed of the lunge.

1. Long legs for wading in water depths of about 10 inches (25 cm).

American Flamingo | *Phoenicopterus ruber*

Rare nonbreeding visitor to Southern Florida. Casual records elsewhere.

FLAMINGOS ARE RARE BIRDS IN THE UNITED STATES, with the only regular records coming from Southern Florida. The species has never bred, but it was once a frequent migrant from the Bahamas, occurring in large flocks. These days only a handful remains and some might be of captive origin, but others are undoubtedly wild birds wandering up from the South. More dubious individuals turn up from time to time in other parts of the United States.

Most people recognize a Flamingo, with its pink plumage, remarkably long neck and legs, and bizarre bent bill. The strange morphology is related to the Flamingo's lifestyle. It can wade in anything from shallow to meter-deep water and can filter small creatures from the mud down by its feet. When feeding, the head is immersed, upside down and facing backward. The bird draws water into its bill by means of the pumping action of its tongue, and particles are filtered both by the narrow opening of the bill and by a network of small comblike projections on the inner edges of the mandibles.

Flamingos are also famous for their odd nests, which are cones of mud anywhere from 1–1.5 feet (30–40 cm) tall with a slight cup in the middle. They are also noted for the way in which they feed their young in the early days, which is on a form of "milk" secreted from the parents' crop.

10 THINGS TO REMEMBER

1. Long, bare legs allow a flamingo to wade almost up to its belly without soiling feathers.

2. Legs have toes that are partially webbed, allowing the birds to swim at times.

3. Flamingos tend to occur in very saline water, where they feed on a range of small organisms such as shrimps, mollusks, worms, and algae.

4. Strange pink coloration is due to the ingestion of algae which contain special pigments.

5. Exceptionally long neck allows flamingos to feed in a wide range of water depths.

6. The shape of the curious bent bill ensures that, when bill is slightly open, the gap between mandibles is a consistent width (a straight bill would make the opening greater at the tip and smaller at the base).

7. [Inset] The bill never quite shuts, leaving an even gap of .1–.2in (4–6mm) between the mandibles. No particle larger than this can be drawn in.

8. [Inset] Inner edges of mandibles are fitted with small projections that form a mesh to filter out items as small as .01 inch (0.5 mm).

9. Birds often turn their head from side to side to communicate—this display is called "flagging."

10. Long wings allow for strong flight, needed for commuting between foraging and breeding sites.

6. The shape of the curious bent bill ensures that, when bill is slightly open, the gap between mandibles is a consistent width (a straight bill would make the opening greater at the tip and smaller at the base).

9. Birds often turn their head from side to side to communicate—this display is called "flagging."

5. Exceptionally long neck allows flamingos to feed in a wide range of water depths.

4. Strange pink coloration is due to the ingestion of algae which contain special pigments.

10. Long wings allow for strong flight, needed for commuting between foraging and breeding sites.

7. The bill never quite shuts, leaving an even gap of .1–.2in (4–6mm) between the mandibles. No particle larger than this can be drawn in.

1. Long, bare legs allow a flamingo to wade almost up to its belly without soiling feathers.

3. Flamingos tend to occur in very saline water, where they feed on a range of small organisms such as shrimps, mollusks, worms, and algae.

8. Inner edges of mandibles are fitted with small projections that form a mesh to filter out items as small as .01 inch (0.5 mm).

2. Legs have toes that are partially webbed, allowing the birds to swim at times.

California Condor | *Gymnogyps californianus*

Reintroduced populations are present all year in Southern California and in the region of the Grand Canyon in Arizona.

THE CALIFORNIA CONDOR IS PROBABLY MOST FAMOUS for being one of North America's rarest birds. In the late Pleistocene, it was common all over the continent, feeding alongside other great vulture species on the carcasses of mammoths, horses, bison, and camels. However, 10,000 years ago the climate cooled and the Condor retreated to the far West. Human persecution drove it to near extinction, so that by 1987 it occurred only in zoos. Since then, successful captive breeding programs have established new free-living populations in places such as the Grand Canyon.

The Condor is a scavenger, dependent on eating the bodies of dead animals. This lifestyle involves hour upon hour of surveillance on the wing, riding thermals over vast distances, watching the ground below for signs of death. Since they feed mainly on large carcasses which are invariably scarce—domestic animals, deer, mountain lions, and, on the coast, sea lions—Condors are able to go for weeks without food if necessary. When hunting, they often monitor the activities of smaller scavengers, such as Turkey Vultures, and follow these down to kills. Their sheer bulk allows them dominance and first pick of the dead flesh.

10 THINGS TO REMEMBER

1. Huge wingspread of over 9 feet (2.8 m), the largest of any North American bird.

2. Very long and broad wings allow the Condor to soar for many hours on updrafts and thermals without using much energy.

3. Slots in wings help to reduce turbulence at wing tip.

4. [Inset] Naked face is necessary for a bird that puts its head into dead flesh. Feathers on the head would get soiled and dirty.

5. [Inset] Color of head and neck changes according to bird's state of arousal. They become brighter in both threat display and courtship.

6. [Inset] Head and neck contain air sacs that become inflated during disputes.

7. The bill is long and hooked, to tear flesh.

8. Claws are unusually short and not used for killing.

9. The large white patch on the underwing shows that this is an adult Condor (gray in youngsters).

10. Condors usually soar several hundred feet in the air when searching for food, keeping watch on the landscape and other scavengers. They often use mountain updrafts to maintain lift.

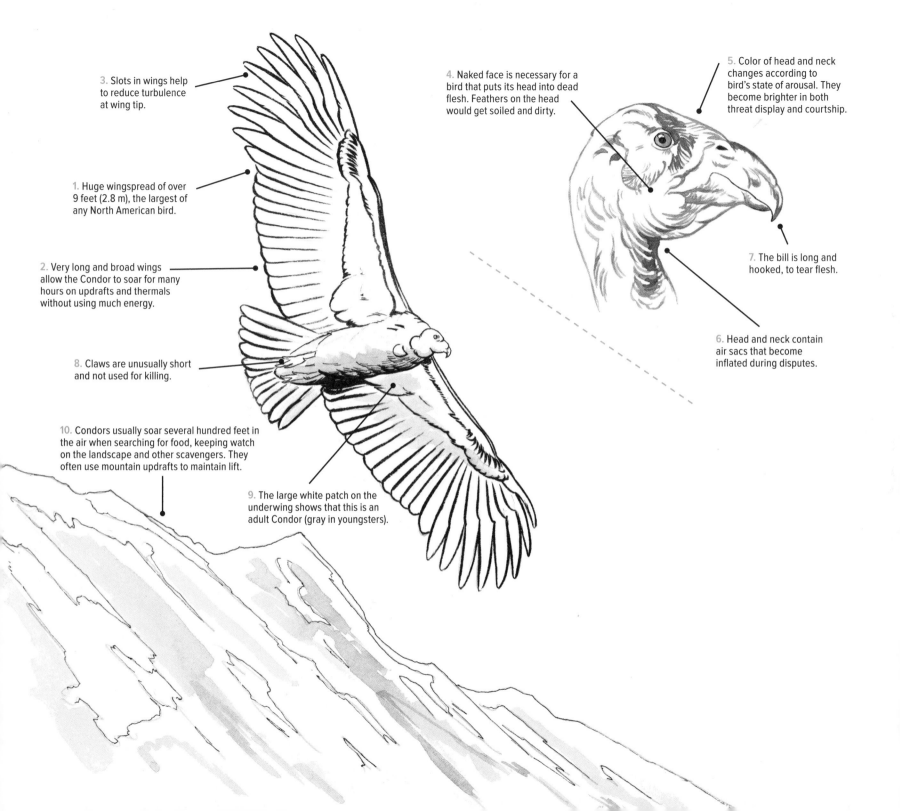

3. Slots in wings help to reduce turbulence at wing tip.

1. Huge wingspread of over 9 feet (2.8 m), the largest of any North American bird.

2. Very long and broad wings allow the Condor to soar for many hours on updrafts and thermals without using much energy.

8. Claws are unusually short and not used for killing.

10. Condors usually soar several hundred feet in the air when searching for food, keeping watch on the landscape and other scavengers. They often use mountain updrafts to maintain lift.

9. The large white patch on the underwing shows that this is an adult Condor (gray in youngsters).

4. Naked face is necessary for a bird that puts its head into dead flesh. Feathers on the head would get soiled and dirty.

5. Color of head and neck changes according to bird's state of arousal. They become brighter in both threat display and courtship.

7. The bill is long and hooked, to tear flesh.

6. Head and neck contain air sacs that become inflated during disputes.

Sharp-shinned Hawk | *Accipiter striatus*

In forests and hills, breeds from Alaska and most of Canada south of the Hudson Bay, extending south in the United States to the Appalachian region and the Rockies. In the Prairies and south, it's mainly a winter visitor, but it can be seen on migration almost anywhere.

NOT ALWAYS THE MOST POPULAR VISITOR TO BACKYARDS, the Sharp-shinned Hawk is a common predator to small birds throughout the North American continent. It has been recorded taking birds of all sizes from the tiny Anna's Hummingbird to the Ruffed Grouse, which is larger than the raptor itself. The hawk also takes occasional mammals and insects, but 90 percent of its diet is avian.

This small hunter is a stealth predator. It spends much of its time concealed among foliage, watching the comings and goings of prey species. Once an attack has been planned, it will set off from its perch, accelerating toward the target with a few powerful flaps of its wings. It will attempt to keep concealed until the last moment, often using objects such as trees, fences, cars, or even people as a screen, until it finally strikes with its feet, keeping its eyes fixed on the moving target. The prey is usually killed by the talons, before being dragged to a perch where it is plucked before eating.

Young birds are easier to catch than experienced adults, so the Sharp-shinned Hawk nests late in the season, sometimes laying eggs in June, so that there will be many juvenile chickadees or blackbirds around in the summer on which it can feed its growing young. It nests in a tree, usually a conifer, and lays 4–5 eggs.

10 THINGS TO REMEMBER

1. Very sharp, hooked bill for tearing flesh and biting back of neck if prey needs to be killed.
2. Large eyes have wide view for catching highly maneuverable prey. They see more detail than human eyes.
3. Eyes are set forward to help it judge distance.
4. Long, curved claws are sharp for killing prey.
5. Long legs give the bird wide reach.
6. Tarsus (leg) is laterally compressed, hence the name "Sharp-shinned" Hawk.
7. Middle claw of the front three is the longest, to increase reach of claws.
8. Long tail for agile flight and sharp braking.
9. Wings are relatively short and broad for a raptor, ideal for rapid acceleration.
10. Chickadees are a very common food source. The Sharp-shinned Hawk is a small predator and mostly eats songbirds.

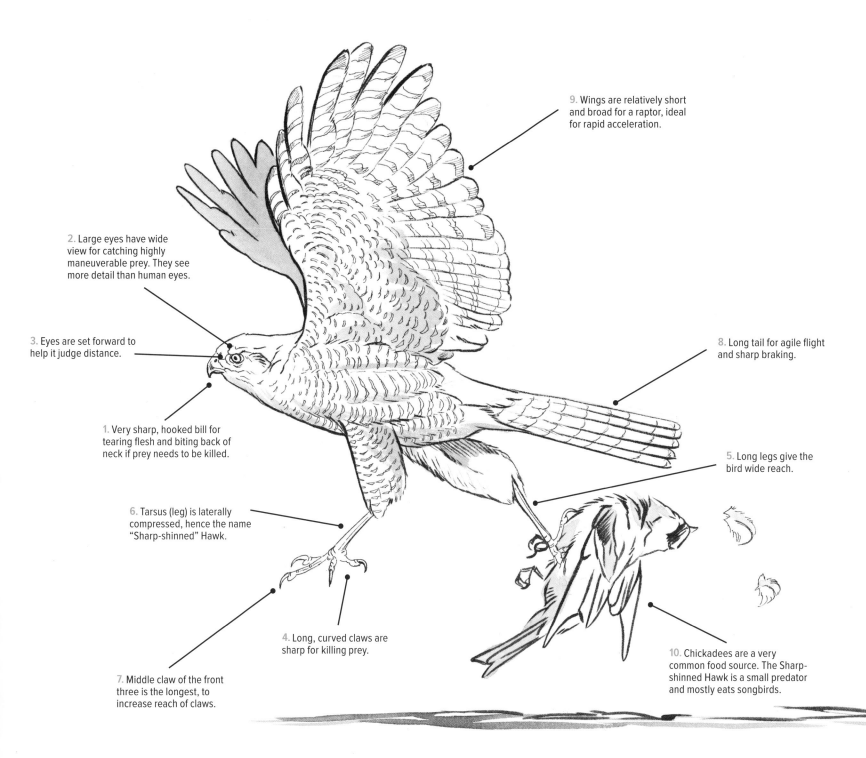

9. Wings are relatively short and broad for a raptor, ideal for rapid acceleration.

2. Large eyes have wide view for catching highly maneuverable prey. They see more detail than human eyes.

3. Eyes are set forward to help it judge distance.

8. Long tail for agile flight and sharp braking.

1. Very sharp, hooked bill for tearing flesh and biting back of neck if prey needs to be killed.

5. Long legs give the bird wide reach.

6. Tarsus (leg) is laterally compressed, hence the name "Sharp-shinned" Hawk.

4. Long, curved claws are sharp for killing prey.

10. Chickadees are a very common food source. The Sharp-shinned Hawk is a small predator and mostly eats songbirds.

7. Middle claw of the front three is the longest, to increase reach of claws.

Peregrine Falcon | *Falco peregrinus*

Present all year in Alaska and northern Canada east to Baffin Island; also can be found in parts of the Rockies, the Pacific Coast, and in localized areas of the United States, often urban in distribution.

FEW BIRDS IN THE WORLD INSPIRE MORE RESPECT and awe than the super-fast Peregrine Falcon, the master of the air. It is, quite simply, the world's supreme self-powered animal, able to attain speeds of at least 112 mph (180 km/h) when diving down from a height onto prey, and regularly attains 62 mph (100 km/h) in level flight. In the wild, its effortless accelerations, twists, and turns are nothing less than a marvel.

A less well-known, but equally impressive statistic is that the Peregrine Falcon is also one of the world's most widely distributed birds. Apart from North America, it also occurs in every continent apart from the Antarctic, in every climatic zone from the extreme Arctic to deserts, and from sea level to high mountains. There are few habitats that don't suit the Peregrine Falcon, as long as there are birds to eat and a ledge on which to nest. It has been recorded eating hundreds of species of birds, possibly even a thousand in total—one tenth of all the bird species in the world.

Peregrine Falcons are broadly but patchily distributed in North America. They are most common in the Far North, including Alaska and the Canadian tundra, but are also widespread in the Rockies. A more unexpected center of distribution is in urban areas in the northern and central states, where the birds nest on tall buildings in such cities as New York, Chicago, and Milwaukee. Individual birds in these areas feed mainly on pigeons. It is therefore possible to observe Peregrines stooping and making their high-speed, ruthless kills, even above the teeming traffic and bustling crowds of urban streets.

DID YOU KNOW?

The stoop can begin when the Falcon is over a mile (2 km) away from the target.

10 THINGS TO REMEMBER

1. Its prey are captured by a head-first dive from high in the air, a maneuver known as a "stoop."

2. Wings are held close to the body to reduce drag.

3. At the last moment, the talons are brought down to strike the prey.

4. The Peregrine Falcon is "chest-heavy" because of its very large, powerful flight muscles.

5. It has a streamlined body for fast movement through the air.

6. Sharp wing tips cut down air resistance to increase speed.

7. Nasal opening or "cere." Inside are cones on the inside that break up wind flow, allowing the bird to breathe even when traveling fast.

8. Eyes are set to an angle of 40 degrees on either side of the bill—this means that the birds have a wide range of vision. It also means that, when stooping, the Peregrine doesn't go straight toward its prey, but at a slight angle.

9. The underside is whitish, making the bird hard to see from below.

10. Dark markings around eyes reduce glare.

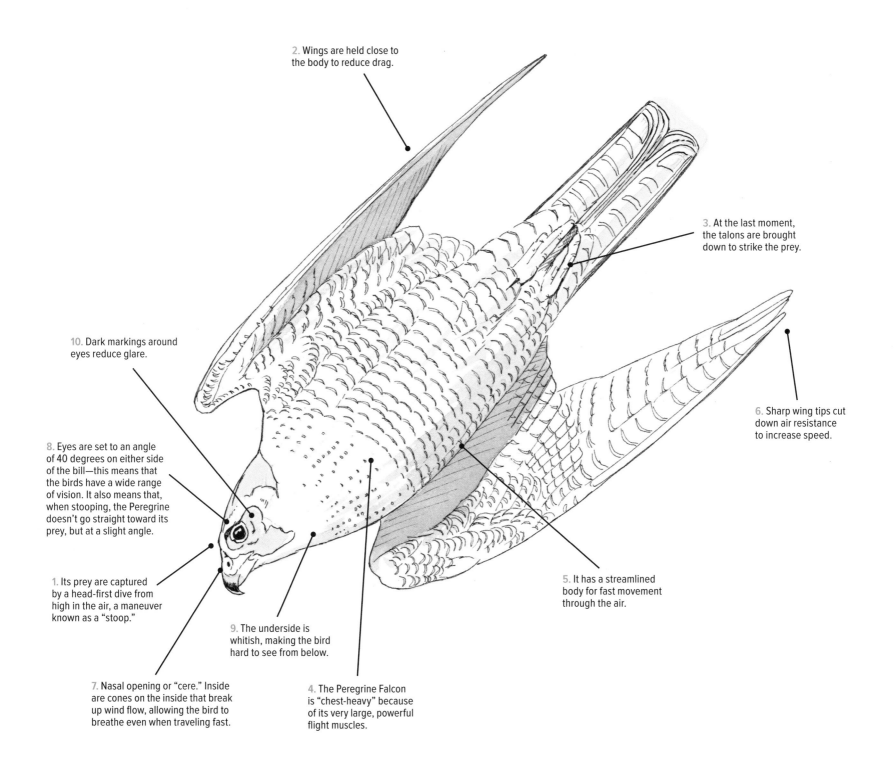

2. Wings are held close to the body to reduce drag.

3. At the last moment, the talons are brought down to strike the prey.

10. Dark markings around eyes reduce glare.

6. Sharp wing tips cut down air resistance to increase speed.

8. Eyes are set to an angle of 40 degrees on either side of the bill—this means that the birds have a wide range of vision. It also means that, when stooping, the Peregrine doesn't go straight toward its prey, but at a slight angle.

5. It has a streamlined body for fast movement through the air.

1. Its prey are captured by a head-first dive from high in the air, a maneuver known as a "stoop."

9. The underside is whitish, making the bird hard to see from below.

7. Nasal opening or "cere." Inside are cones on the inside that break up wind flow, allowing the bird to breathe even when traveling fast.

4. The Peregrine Falcon is "chest-heavy" because of its very large, powerful flight muscles.

Rock Ptarmigan | *Lagopus muta*

They can be found through much of Alaska and the Aleutians to the east across extreme northern Canada, including offshore islands and Greenland; there is an isolated population in Newfoundland, and they can also be found in British Columbia and the Yukon Territory.

NO LAND BIRD IN THE WORLD OCCURS AT HIGHER LATITUDES than the remarkable Rock Ptarmigan, a species that can endure the very worst storms that the Arctic can throw at it. Occurring on the tundra high above the tree line, it has been recorded above 80°N in Greenland, even in the midst of winter. In such conditions it is kept insulated by its thick plumage that extends all the way to the feet and toes, while the bird itself feeds on vegetation under the snow, foodstuffs that can be found even during the dark days. With its long gut, it can extract nutrition even from needles, twigs, and other meager offerings.

The Rock Ptarmigan is famous for its plumage changes, which reflect its immediate environment. In the winter, when snow covers its tundra habitat, the bird turns almost completely white (but for black on the tail and, in the male, the face). In spring, the plumage is brown with blotches of white; and then in late summer, it goes grayish to provide camouflage against the fading colors of the tundra vegetation. Apart from this and the two other species of Ptarmigans, no other bird in the world has three molts in a year.

10 THINGS TO REMEMBER

1. (L) White plumage of both sexes in winter (October–April) helps to camouflage birds against the snow.

2. Plumage is very thick, especially in winter, and helps, along with fat deposits, to keep bird insulated in its Arctic environment.

3. Legs are feathered to maintain insulation.

4. [Inset] Feet and toes are also feathered. This not only insulates, but it gives the bird "snowshoes," allowing it to walk easily on the snow surface.

5. (L) Red combs over eyes are prominent in males and can be inflated. Male-to-male attacks are directed to the combs. Displays take place when the birds have white plumage.

6. (M) In spring (April–June), only a few white blotches remain. Rest of plumage is cryptic against grayish rocks of habitat.

7. (R) In summer (July–September), the Rock Ptarmigan acquires another cryptic plumage to reflect the fading colors of the tundra vegetation.

8. The bird is usually found in rocky places with sparse vegetation and feeds on the ground.

9. Plump body includes long gut for digesting even the least nutritious vegetation.

10. Small but sharp bill used for browsing on vegetation. Buds, for example, are held in tip of the bill and removed by a quick, sideways turn of the head.

Left (L) – male in winter
Middle (M) – male in spring
Right (R)– male in summer
Plus Close-up (Inset) of feet

4. Feet and toes are also feathered. This not only insulates, but it gives the bird "snowshoes," allowing it to walk easily on the snow surface.

10. Small but sharp bill used for browsing on vegetation. Buds, for example, are held in tip of the bill and removed by a quick, sideways turn of the head.

6. In spring (April–June), only a few white blotches remain. Rest of plumage is cryptic against grayish rocks of habitat.

5. Red combs over eyes are prominent in males and can be inflated. Male-to-male attacks are directed to the combs. Displays take place when the birds have white plumage.

7. In summer (July–September), the Rock Ptarmigan acquires another cryptic plumage to reflect the fading colors of the tundra vegetation.

2. Plumage is very thick, especially in winter, and helps, along with fat deposits, to keep bird insulated in its Arctic environment.

9. Plump body includes long gut for digesting even the least nutritious vegetation.

8. The bird is usually found in rocky places with sparse vegetation and feeds on the ground.

1. White plumage of both sexes in winter (October–April) helps to camouflage birds against the snow.

3. Legs are feathered to maintain insulation.

Greater Sage-Grouse | *Centrocercus urophasianus*

Present all year in sage country of the West, mainly in Oregon, California, Idaho, Nevada, Utah, Colorado, Wyoming, Montana, North and South Dakota, Alberta, Saskatchewan, and Washington.

TRUE TO ITS NAME, THE SAGE-GROUSE is found only in the sagebrush (*Artemesia*) dominated ecosystems of the interior west. Its dependence on these habitats is complete. It nests within sagebrush and all individual birds depend for their nourishment on the leaves and fresh shoots of sagebrush throughout the fall, winter, and into early spring. Without this plant, the Sage-Grouse would simply not exist.

Aside from its association with this one particular type of plant, the Sage-Grouse is most famous for its spectacular courtship displays, illustrated opposite. They are a classic example of a so-called "lek." A lek is a gathering of displaying males that perform communally in order to attract an audience of females to their show. Once arrived, females can observe all the males present on a site and make a choice as to which bird they wish to copulate with. However, the choice is partly made for them, because the males at a lek (and there may be 70 of them) compete among themselves for the central position within the display ground. The winners are self-evidently the quality birds, and within a lek, it is usually just one or two males that enjoy the lion's share of copulations.

To our eyes, the display of the Greater Sage-Grouse is truly spectacular. The bird puffs out its chest, lets its wings droop, inflates yellow air sacs, and raises and spreads its tail. As the air sacs deflate, they add a loud popping sound to the overall effect, making it one of the most diverting spectacles among North American birds.

10 THINGS TO REMEMBER

1. Spiky tail feathers spread fanlike in display.

2. The broad, rounded wings are drooped during display. The Sage-Grouse is a powerful flier, able to rocket away at nearly 50mph (78km/h).

3. The birds have very short legs, which aren't good for running.

4. The heavy body is typical of the Grouse family.

5. It thrusts out a puffy white chest in display.

6. Two large orange air sacs, which are usually invisible as bare patches on the breast, inflate like balloons and deflate with a pop.

7. Yellow fleshy comb over eye.

8. The plumes on the head are known as "filoplumes"; they are raised in display.

9. Short, thick bill with cutting edge for eating leaves and other vegetable matter.

10. Males display at a lek on open ground near to sagebrush. Males display in the very early morning, and communally, so they will not be seen alone.

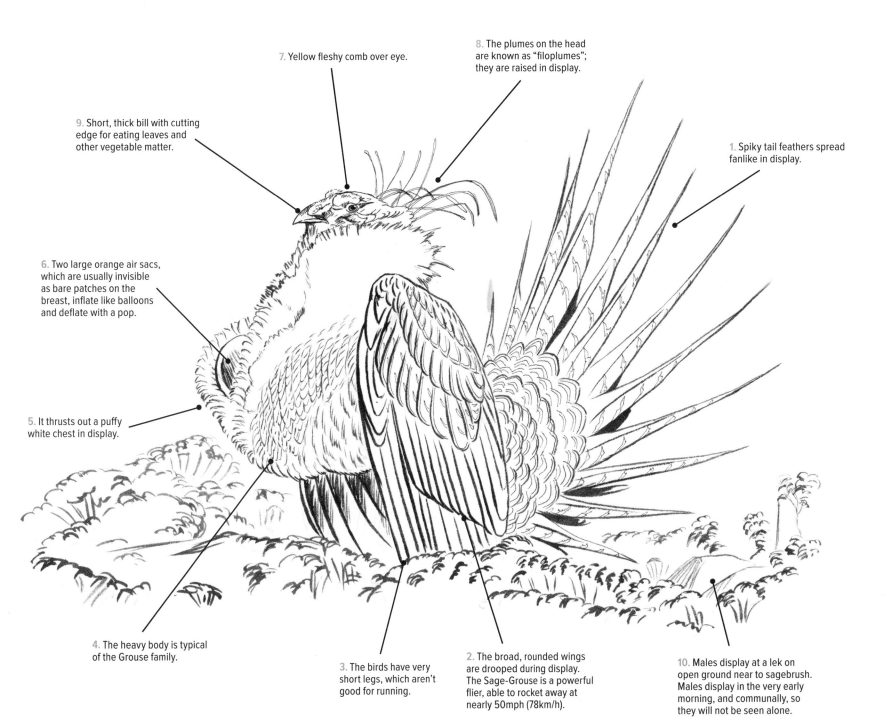

7. Yellow fleshy comb over eye.

8. The plumes on the head are known as "filoplumes"; they are raised in display.

1. Spiky tail feathers spread fanlike in display.

9. Short, thick bill with cutting edge for eating leaves and other vegetable matter.

6. Two large orange air sacs, which are usually invisible as bare patches on the breast, inflate like balloons and deflate with a pop.

5. It thrusts out a puffy white chest in display.

4. The heavy body is typical of the Grouse family.

3. The birds have very short legs, which aren't good for running.

2. The broad, rounded wings are drooped during display. The Sage-Grouse is a powerful flier, able to rocket away at nearly 50mph (78km/h).

10. Males display at a lek on open ground near to sagebrush. Males display in the very early morning, and communally, so they will not be seen alone.

Northern Jacana | *Jacana spinosa*

A sporadic winter visitor to southern Texas.

A RARE BIRD IN THE UNITED STATES, THE NORTHERN JACANA is found only sporadically in Texas, being more common in Mexico. It comes from a family of shorebirds found mainly in the tropics. It occurs in rich, well-vegetated freshwater marshes.

Jacanas are best known for their remarkably elongated toes. These spread the bird's weight evenly when it is walking, allowing it to occupy a unique niche habitat—floating vegetation, especially water lily pads. These birds can live and forage on this fragile habitat, rich in animal life. The birds even build their nests on floating vegetation, although lily pads aren't quite robust enough.

The long toes are not the only unusual aspect of the Jacana. Its breeding biology reverses the norm, in that males carry out all the nest-building, incubation, and care of the young. Females, meanwhile, will often mate with several males—up to 4 at a time—and indeed may lay several clutches of eggs for each of them. Females assist the males with holding their own territories, and fights are commonplace. Birds scuffle by jabbing their bills forward and also striking with the angle of the wings, where there is a small spur.

10 THINGS TO REMEMBER

1. Vastly elongated toes spread the Jacana's weight over a wide area, preventing it from sinking when walking.

2. Unique habitat of water lily pads and other floating vegetation.

3. When walking, the Jacana lifts up one foot deliberately at a time to ensure its feet don't get tangled. Other birds have foot movements that tend to overlap more.

4. Before it places its foot down, the Jacana spreads its toes first.

5. Long legs allow big steps that prove useful if a foothold gives way.

6. Long bill for stabbing at prey (fish, beetles, snails, and other small animals) and for gleaning from vegetation.

7. Bright yellow shield on forehead. Size and fleshiness varies hormonally, and females have larger shields than males.

8. The short, rounded wings indicate that Jacanas are not strong fliers.

9. The spur on angle of wing is frequently used in fighting.

10. Brown coloration conceals bird from predators.

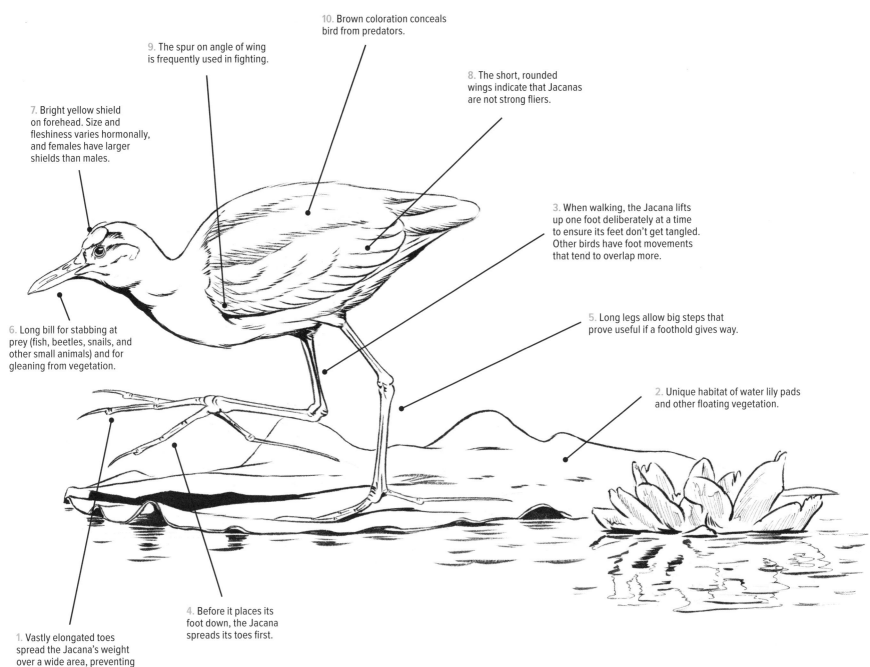

10. Brown coloration conceals bird from predators.

9. The spur on angle of wing is frequently used in fighting.

8. The short, rounded wings indicate that Jacanas are not strong fliers.

7. Bright yellow shield on forehead. Size and fleshiness varies hormonally, and females have larger shields than males.

3. When walking, the Jacana lifts up one foot deliberately at a time to ensure its feet don't get tangled. Other birds have foot movements that tend to overlap more.

6. Long bill for stabbing at prey (fish, beetles, snails, and other small animals) and for gleaning from vegetation.

5. Long legs allow big steps that prove useful if a foothold gives way.

2. Unique habitat of water lily pads and other floating vegetation.

1. Vastly elongated toes spread the Jacana's weight over a wide area, preventing it from sinking when walking.

4. Before it places its foot down, the Jacana spreads its toes first.

American Golden Plover | *Pluvialis dominica*

Breeds in tundra from Alaska eastwards across the Yukon and Northwest Territories and Nunavut as far as the shore of Hudson Bay in Manitoba; a few can also be found in Ontario. Uncommon spring and autumn migrant south of here.

A SMART INHABITANT OF THE ARCTIC AND SUB-ARCTIC TUNDRA of North America, the Golden Plover is a powerful and durable bird. Besides coping with its harsh habitat, it is capable of flying at great heights and for extended periods at speeds of up to 85 mph (136 km/h).

Plovers have a very specific feeding method that separates them from other shorebirds. Rather than probing into mud or grass, using their sense of touch to detect items in the substrate, they find most of their food by surveillance. Thus they are often seen standing still, only to break into a short run after a while, either to run toward food they have spotted, or to switch vantage points. A Plover's movement, therefore, is distinctively stop-start, and can be used to distinguish them from other shorebirds feeding nearby.

One of the most extraordinary aspects of the Golden Plover's lifestyle is its migration. From the tundra of North America, it migrates in the fall to the grasslands of southern South America, especially Argentina and Uruguay. It is one of the longest migrations known of any bird, often exceeding 9,000 miles (15,000 km). Individuals can probably exceed over 4,000 miles (7,000 km) in a single flight, traveling at a high altitude to use strong tailwinds.

10 THINGS TO REMEMBER

1. Tongue is used to hold food in the bill (this is a general rule among birds).

2. Relatively short and thick bill for a shorebird—this is typical of a bird that feeds at the surface, rather than probing into the mud.

3. Their large eyes enable them to hunt by sight rather than touch, and they can even forage in moonlight.

4. Long legs elevate the Plover to allow for a good view of its immediate surroundings.

5. The "knees" of a bird are in fact not equivalent to our knees, but are the tibio-tarsal joint—equivalent to our ankles.

6. The Plover often calls (a whistle) while on the ground to intruders overhead, showing that its territory is occupied.

7. Bold black breast plumage is ruffled during courtship displays.

8. Upper parts, including the back, wings, hindneck, and crown, are cryptically patterned and look like tundra vegetation.

9. The hind toe is absent, which helps the bird to run with minimal effort.

10. Long wings allow exceptional speed and durability in the air.

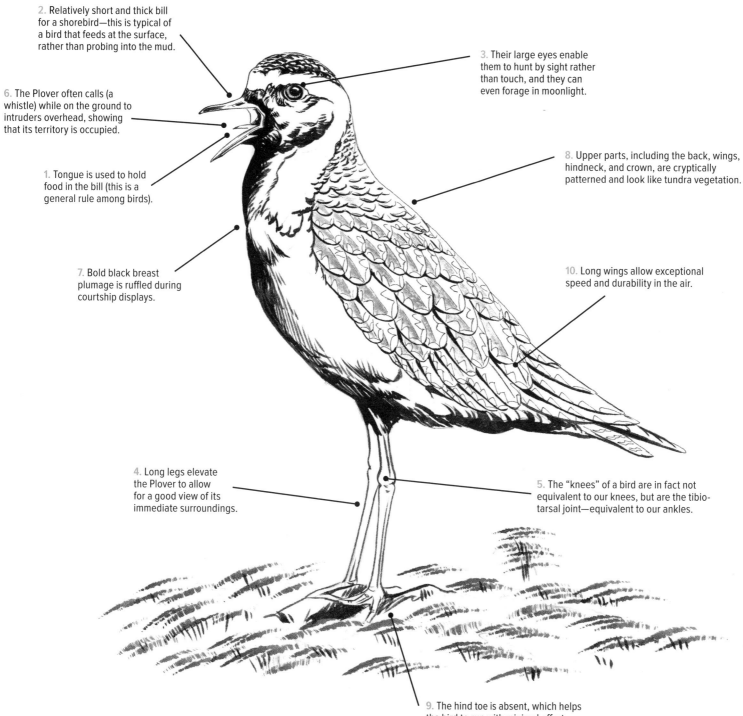

2. Relatively short and thick bill for a shorebird—this is typical of a bird that feeds at the surface, rather than probing into the mud.

6. The Plover often calls (a whistle) while on the ground to intruders overhead, showing that its territory is occupied.

1. Tongue is used to hold food in the bill (this is a general rule among birds).

7. Bold black breast plumage is ruffled during courtship displays.

3. Their large eyes enable them to hunt by sight rather than touch, and they can even forage in moonlight.

8. Upper parts, including the back, wings, hindneck, and crown, are cryptically patterned and look like tundra vegetation.

10. Long wings allow exceptional speed and durability in the air.

4. Long legs elevate the Plover to allow for a good view of its immediate surroundings.

5. The "knees" of a bird are in fact not equivalent to our knees, but are the tibio-tarsal joint—equivalent to our ankles.

9. The hind toe is absent, which helps the bird to run with minimal effort.

American Avocet | *Recurvirostra americana*

Breeds locally in most western and Midwestern states, with high numbers in Utah and Idaho. Winters mainly south of the United States.

THE STRIKING AND UNUSUAL AMERICAN AVOCET is found in shallow inland ponds, marshes, and lakeshores in the breeding season and on lagoons and seashores in the fall and winter. The American Avocet is unique in that it feeds in water that is much too deep for other shorebirds. Here it either wades on its extremely long legs, or swims. It can find food both by sight, picking items off the water surface, or more typically by touch. The most typical "touch" method is to make its bill cut through the water by swaying it from side to side, a technique known as "scything." As soon as the hypersensitive mandibles touch something edible in the water column, the Avocet can grab it. In this way, Avocets eat insects and their larvae, crustaceans, and small fish.

American Avocets tend to be sociable birds, both feeding in groups and breeding in colonies. They select open ground for their nests, often on an island in a marsh, where they lay eggs on the soft mud, frequently in areas with some sparse ground vegetation. Pairs are assiduous in defending their eggs or young, aggressively and noisily. The young can swim from an early age and dive to evade capture. Some flightless chicks have been recorded swimming 23 feet (7 m) underwater.

10 THINGS TO REMEMBER

1. Unusual blue legs are very long, enabling the bird to wade deeply.

2. Bill is uptilted. Bird often feeds by swaying a slightly open bill ("scything") from side to side in the water.

3. Angle of uptilt is such that, when the bird leans down to feed, the maximum horizontal length of the bill is immersed.

4. Long neck enables the American Avocet to reach down to feed.

5. In common with other touch-feeding shorebirds, the bill is covered with millions of tactile receptors that allow the bird to detect food in the water column.

6. The American Avocet typically wades in moderately deep water 6–8 inches (15–20 cm), too deep for most other shorebirds.

7. Webbing of toes allows the Avocet to swim well.

8. Slim body allows bird to fly rapidly when needed.

9. Salmon-pink color on neck turns to gray in nonbreeding season.

10. Bold black-and-white coloration is probably disruptive camouflage, breaking up the shape of the bird.

10. Bold black-and-white coloration is probably disruptive camouflage, breaking up the shape of the bird.

9. Salmon-pink color on neck turns to gray in nonbreeding season.

5. In common with other touch-feeding shorebirds, the bill is covered with millions of tactile receptors that allow the bird to detect food in the water column.

2. Bill is uptilted. Bird often feeds by swaying a slightly open bill ("scything") from side to side in the water.

8. Slim body allows bird to fly rapidly when needed.

3. Angle of uptilt is such that, when the bird leans down to feed, the maximum horizontal length of the bill is immersed.

4. Long neck enables the bird to reach down to feed.

1. Unusual blue legs are very long, enabling the bird to wade deeply.

7. Webbing of toes allows the Avocet to swim well.

6. The American Avocet typically wades in moderately deep water 6–8 inches (15–20 cm), too deep for most other shorebirds.

Bar-tailed Godwit | *Limosa lapponica*

Breeds only in north and west Alaska. Rarely seen in migration to the Atlantic and Pacific coasts.

THIS UNASSUMING SHOREBIRD, RARE IN NORTH AMERICA, holds one of the most remarkable avian records—the longest single flight, without touching down, of any non-seabird. The Bar-tailed Godwits have been radio-tracked on their fall migration from the tundra of Alaska, across the Pacific Ocean to New Zealand. Birds undertaking this journey covered at least 6,462 miles (10,400 km) without stopping, or indeed being able to stop, and the continuous flight took them just over a week. It is a truly astonishing feat, not just of endurance but of navigation, too. And there is no doubt that these birds have been doing the same flight for countless generations.

The Bar-tailed Godwit is mostly a bird of the Old World, occurring on tundra across Siberia. In Alaska, it breeds especially on wet meadows that contain some dwarf shrub. It makes a shallow scrape on the ground for its nest and lays 4 eggs. The adults are famously aggressive in defense of their brood, and will fearlessly attack any animal or bird predator that threatens them.

The Godwit's long, slightly upturned bill is used for probing into soft substrates such as the mud of estuaries. When feeding, this shorebird relies largely upon its sense of touch to find such items as shellfish, worms, and crustaceans that are hidden in the ooze. It can feed in low light conditions when necessary, and can also gather in tight-knit flocks without each individual interfering with the foraging of its neighbor.

10 THINGS TO REMEMBER

1. Long legs for wading, if necessary, in bog or estuarine habitat.
2. Hind toe is raised. With fewer bones on the ground, resistance is reduced, and the bird can run faster.
3. Tarsus is partially feathered, for protection and to reduce heat loss through the legs.
4. Dull coloration of nonbreeding plumage allows for camouflage against mud and seashore. When breeding, the plumage is a bright reddish color.
5. Long neck for reaching down to probe for food.
6. The Bar-tailed Godwit has relatively smaller eyes than a Plover, reflecting its reliance on the sense of touch over sight.
7. Long, slightly uptilted bill can probe deep into mud.
8. Tip of the bill is covered with various kinds of touch receptors, including those that detect shear (stress applied at an angle to the bill) and direct pressure perpendicular to the bill.
9. Primary feathers, also known as primaries, form wing tip.
10. Tertial feathers, also known as tertials, cover folded wing at rest.

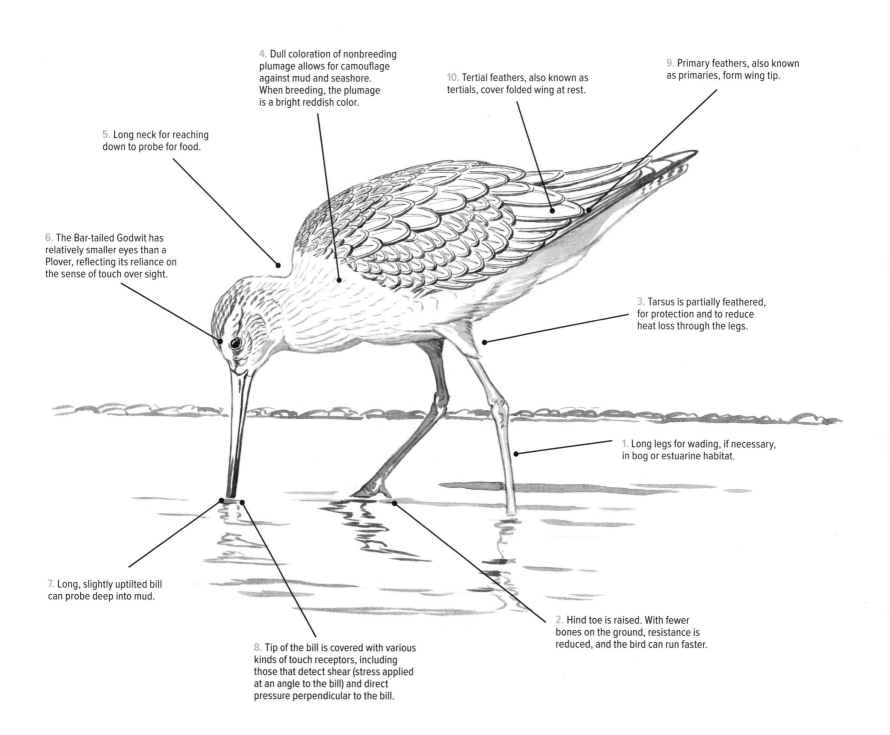

4. Dull coloration of nonbreeding plumage allows for camouflage against mud and seashore. When breeding, the plumage is a bright reddish color.

10. Tertial feathers, also known as tertials, cover folded wing at rest.

9. Primary feathers, also known as primaries, form wing tip.

5. Long neck for reaching down to probe for food.

6. The Bar-tailed Godwit has relatively smaller eyes than a Plover, reflecting its reliance on the sense of touch over sight.

3. Tarsus is partially feathered, for protection and to reduce heat loss through the legs.

1. Long legs for wading, if necessary, in bog or estuarine habitat.

7. Long, slightly uptilted bill can probe deep into mud.

8. Tip of the bill is covered with various kinds of touch receptors, including those that detect shear (stress applied at an angle to the bill) and direct pressure perpendicular to the bill.

2. Hind toe is raised. With fewer bones on the ground, resistance is reduced, and the bird can run faster.

Ruddy Turnstone | *Arenaria interpres*

Breeds on coasts from western Alaska through the Yukon and Northwest Territories, then on the Arctic islands, including Greenland. Winters commonly on both coasts, mainly south of northern California on the Pacific side, and south of Massachusetts on the Atlantic side.

A SINGLE OBSERVATION CAN SUM UP THE RUDDY TURNSTONE and offer an insight into its ecology. If you're watching a flock feeding on a rocky shore on either coast, you will soon see birds stooping down, inserting their bills under the base of an object (like a rock or a weed) and, with a flick of the bill, turning it over or nudging it aside. Once the birds have done so, whatever edible item is revealed below is very much theirs; no other shorebird has access to it. If you've seen this occur, then you have witnessed the feeding habits of the Ruddy Turnstone.

Turnstones are sociable birds when not breeding, and live in small, stable flocks in which individuals maintain a strict hierarchy, with the dominant birds always foraging in the most profitable places. Sometimes, however, a more cooperative mood breaks out, and several individuals may band together to heave a particularly large item over and share the spoils.

Turnstones have a broad diet encompassing not just the normal foodstuffs you might associate with a shorebird, such as crustaceans, mollusks, and worms, but have also been recorded eating soap, scraps, carrion, and even a human corpse. They will also sometimes raid the nests of other birds for eggs.

Ruddy Turnstones breed on the Arctic tundra of the far north.

DID YOU KNOW?

Turnstones are extremely aggressive and will occasionally kill members of the feeding flock if they violate the strict hierarchy.

10 THINGS TO REMEMBER

1. Ruddy Turnstones have plump shapes, with strong, thick necks.
2. Their typical habitat is close to the splash zone of a rocky shore with seaweed and pools.
3. The dark, patchy coloration on this bird is ideal for camouflage among rocks.
4. Short, sharp bill is capable of stripping tissue off carrion.
5. Bill slightly uptilted to help reach under an item the bird wants to move.
6. When feeding, this bird is able to turn over items such as rocks, stones, weeds, or flotsam in order to reveal edible items hidden below.
7. In the nonbreeding season, Ruddy Turnstones can be found in small flocks with a stable membership, in which all the individuals know each other.
8. Face markings are individually variable.
9. Short legs allow birds to get down easily to the base of item and to begin turning it over.
10. This bird's toes are not webbed, so it doesn't wade or swim.

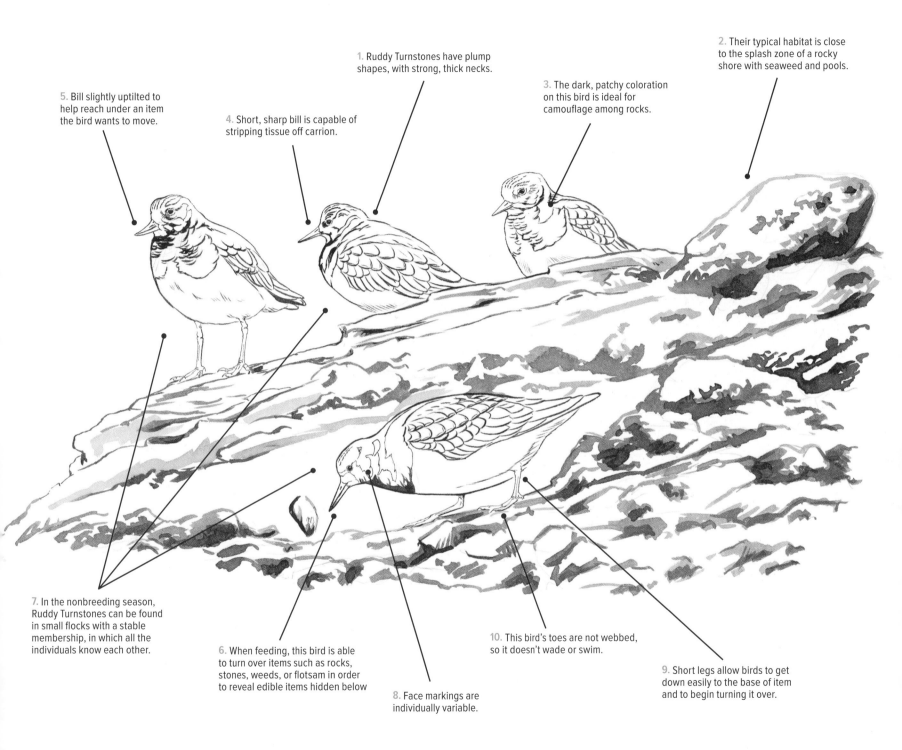

5. Bill slightly uptilted to help reach under an item the bird wants to move.

4. Short, sharp bill is capable of stripping tissue off carrion.

1. Ruddy Turnstones have plump shapes, with strong, thick necks.

3. The dark, patchy coloration on this bird is ideal for camouflage among rocks.

2. Their typical habitat is close to the splash zone of a rocky shore with seaweed and pools.

7. In the nonbreeding season, Ruddy Turnstones can be found in small flocks with a stable membership, in which all the individuals know each other.

6. When feeding, this bird is able to turn over items such as rocks, stones, weeds, or flotsam in order to reveal edible items hidden below

8. Face markings are individually variable.

10. This bird's toes are not webbed, so it doesn't wade or swim.

9. Short legs allow birds to get down easily to the base of item and to begin turning it over.

Wilson's Phalarope | *Phalaropus tricolor*

Breeds locally in a swathe of western and Midwestern states, from British Columbia to Minnesota and Wisconsin, and south to California, Nevada, Utah, Colorado, Wyoming, and North and South Dakota; also in the Great Lakes region. Migrates to South America, but stops over on saline lakes, including Great Salt Lake (UT), Mono Lake (CA), and Stillwater National Wildlife Refuge (NV).

A REAL ODDITY, THE WILSON'S PHALAROPE is a shorebird that prefers to swim, and a breeding bird in which some of the normal behavior between males and females is reversed. It is common on inland marshes in the Midwest, often spending the nonbreeding season on large salt lakes.

The Phalaropes are the most aquatic shorebirds. Instead of walking on mud, or even wading in the water, they are most often seen swimming buoyantly in the water, where they pick at minute items, such as flies and shrimps, from the water surface. A Phalarope often spins on the spot in a peculiar fashion, evidently to stir up food from below the surface, or perhaps to disturb something unseen.

When breeding, the brightly colored female Wilson's Phalaropes are responsible for initiating display and competing for mates, something normally associated in other birds with males. Their males carry out construction of the nest, all incubation of the eggs, and all parental care. Females desert the males once the eggs are laid, and will then often seek another male to promote their productivity.

10 THINGS TO REMEMBER

1. (F) Bold black neck markings. Breeding female is unusual for having brighter and bolder colors than male. Female is responsible for initiating display.

2. (M) Male considerably duller than female, the reverse of the pattern typical for birds. Male alone looks after nest, eggs, and young.

3. (M) Male also slightly smaller than female.

4. Unusual among shorebirds, the Phalaropes swim when feeding.

5. Exceptionally buoyant. Floats on water like a cork.

6. [Inset] Partially lobed feet aid swimming.

7. Favored waters are often hypersaline (very salty), for specialized diet of brine shrimps and brine flies (especially in the nonbreeding season).

8. (M) Has unusual habit of swimming on the spot in circles. This is thought to stir up edible particles in the water.

9. Exceptionally thin bill uses "capillary action" for feeding—surface tension forces water upward through minute gap between mandibles, bringing food to the mouth with it.

10. Long bill allows birds to "pick" at insects and crustaceans from water surface.

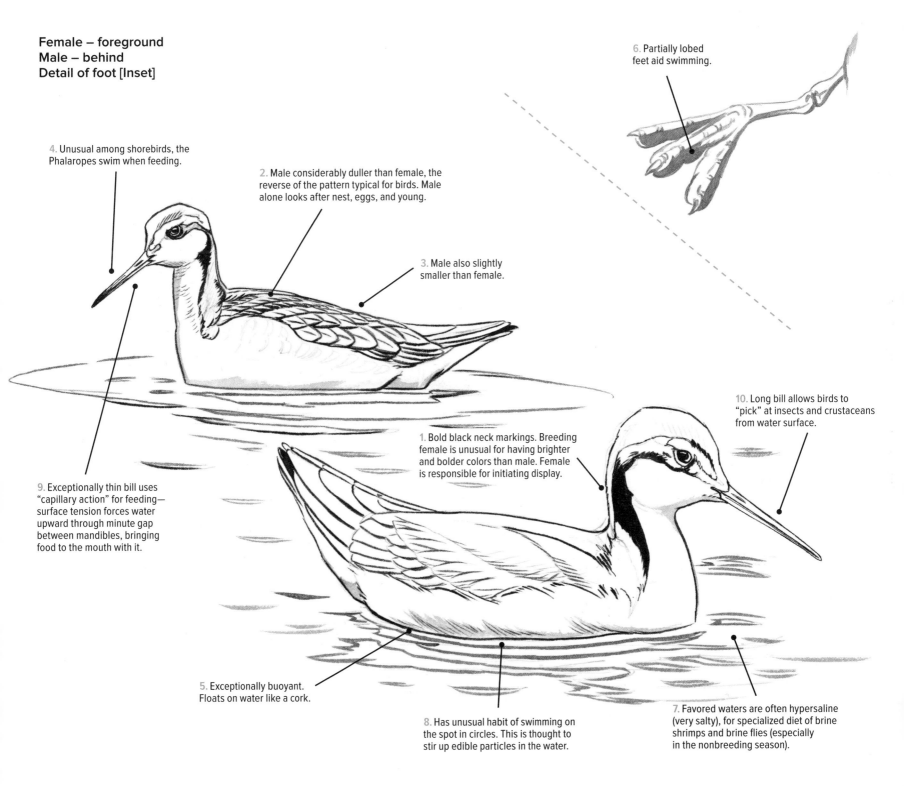

Female – foreground
Male – behind
Detail of foot [Inset]

6. Partially lobed feet aid swimming.

4. Unusual among shorebirds, the Phalaropes swim when feeding.

2. Male considerably duller than female, the reverse of the pattern typical for birds. Male alone looks after nest, eggs, and young.

3. Male also slightly smaller than female.

10. Long bill allows birds to "pick" at insects and crustaceans from water surface.

9. Exceptionally thin bill uses "capillary action" for feeding—surface tension forces water upward through minute gap between mandibles, bringing food to the mouth with it.

1. Bold black neck markings. Breeding female is unusual for having brighter and bolder colors than male. Female is responsible for initiating display.

5. Exceptionally buoyant. Floats on water like a cork.

8. Has unusual habit of swimming on the spot in circles. This is thought to stir up edible particles in the water.

7. Favored waters are often hypersaline (very salty), for specialized diet of brine shrimps and brine flies (especially in the nonbreeding season).

Eastern Screech Owl | *Megascops asio*

Found all year in the eastern half of the United States, south to the Gulf Coast. In Canada, it is mainly found in southern Ontario.

THE QUIET DESCENDING TRILL OF THE EASTERN SCREECH OWL IS A COMMON, if easily overlooked sound of wooded and urban habitats of North America, east of the Rocky Mountains. Birders often imitate the call to elicit a response from small birds, which come to investigate the intrusion.

In truth, birds are only a small part of the Screech Owl's diet: insects and small mammals are much more important and, strangely, fish are a significant prey in some places. Food is located by the owl who sits still below the tree canopy and watches below for movement; if it spots something, the hunter will dive down onto its prey feet-first, usually killing the animal with its talons. Almost all hunting is done at night, using the owl's supreme listening and night-vision capabilities.

Eastern Screech Owls breed in holes in trees and also in nest-boxes. They don't build a nest as such, but just lay 3–4 eggs straight onto the floor of the hole. Some males mate with more than one female.

10 THINGS TO REMEMBER

1. Large eyes help the bird to see well in the dark and large pupils allow for plenty of incoming light.

2. The eyes face forward, like those of humans. The fields of vision of the two eyes overlap, meaning that objects are viewed from two fractionally different viewpoints, and this allows the owl to judge distance effectively.

3. [Inset] The visible "ears" aren't ears at all, but feathered ear tufts. They can be raised and lowered, and they reflect the owl's mood.

4. [Inset] True ears are located on the edges of the facial disc. One ear (the left) is slightly higher up the head than the other, allowing this species three-dimensional hearing.

5. [Inset] Facial disc funnels sound toward the ears, amplifying the signal.

6. The Eastern Screech Owl's large head can be rotated up to 270 degrees in the horizontal plane, allowing the bird to see almost all around without having to turn its body.

7. The hooked bill betrays its predatory lifestyle.

8. Supreme camouflage hides the owl by day.

9. Feathers are extremely soft, dampening any sound made by the bird while flying.

10. Sharp talons kill the prey (usually songbirds, some insects, and occasionally, fish).

1. Large eyes help the bird to see well in the dark and large pupils allow for plenty of incoming light.

2. The eyes face forward, like those of humans. The fields of vision of the two eyes overlap, meaning that objects are viewed from two fractionally different viewpoints, and this allows the owl to judge distance effectively.

3. The visible "ears" aren't ears at all, but feathered ear tufts. They can be raised and lowered, and they reflect the owl's mood.

4. True ears are located on the edges of the facial disc. One ear (the left) is slightly higher up the head than the other, allowing this species three-dimensional hearing.

5. Facial disc funnels sound toward the ears, amplifying the signal.

6. The Eastern Screech Owl's large head can be rotated up to 270 degrees in the horizontal plane, allowing the bird to see almost all around without having to turn its body.

7. The hooked bill betrays its predatory lifestyle.

8. Supreme camouflage hides the owl by day.

9. Feathers are extremely soft, dampening any sound made by the bird while flying.

10. Sharp talons kill the prey (usually songbirds, some insects, and occasionally, fish).

Common Poorwill | *Phalaenoptilus nuttallii*

Breeds in the West from the Canadian border southwards. They are most commonly found in Arizona, California, and parts of Colorado. Northern populations retreat in winter toward Arizona and Mexico.

NOT MANY PEOPLE HAVE SEEN THE COMMON POORWILL, an elusive nocturnal bird of western deserts and grasslands. However, it has always been recognized by the Native Americans of its range, including the Hopi, who named it *Holchöko*, the "Sleeping One." This refers to the Poorwill's extraordinary ability to remain torpid for many days in succession, almost to the point of hibernation. It is estimated that on 90 percent of winter days, when this species' main food supply—flying insects—is unavailable, the Poorwill simply remains at its roost sites, its metabolic rate falling to 10 percent of its active level, measured by oxygen consumption. No other bird in the world spends so much of its life in a comalike state.

When awake, the Poorwill forages by making darting sallies out from a perch, snapping up prey in flight with its large mouth. It captures moths and beetles, mainly those larger than ½ inch (10 mm) long. It feeds at night, at which time the distinctive "Poor-will" call can be heard.

The Poorwill nests on the ground, laying 2 eggs in a shallow scrape. Both sexes incubate the eggs, and when the young hatch, the parents sometimes move them a short distance away, which is a very unusual practice among birds.

10 THINGS TO REMEMBER

1. Extraordinary cryptic plumage makes it almost impossible to see the Poorwill where it roosts by day on the ground.

2. They have large eyes adapted to seeing strong contrast at night, and they have small plates on the retina (*tapetum*) that reflect light back and create eyeshine. This gives light a second opportunity to be detected by receptor cells.

3. The bill is tiny considering the size of the bird, though it is not used for procuring prey.

4. [Inset] The mouth gape on the Poorwill is enormous: it is used to catch prey, like a net.

5. [Inset] Bristles on the side of the mouth act as touch receptors.

6. [Inset] The extraordinarily flexible mouth can be moved sideways and also accommodates relatively large prey.

7. The bird typically sits on the ground lengthways. It has very small feet and does not usually perch across branches.

8. Its soft plumage allows the Poorwill to fly silently.

9. The long wings confer good aerial maneuverability.

10. This particular species has an extremely short neck.

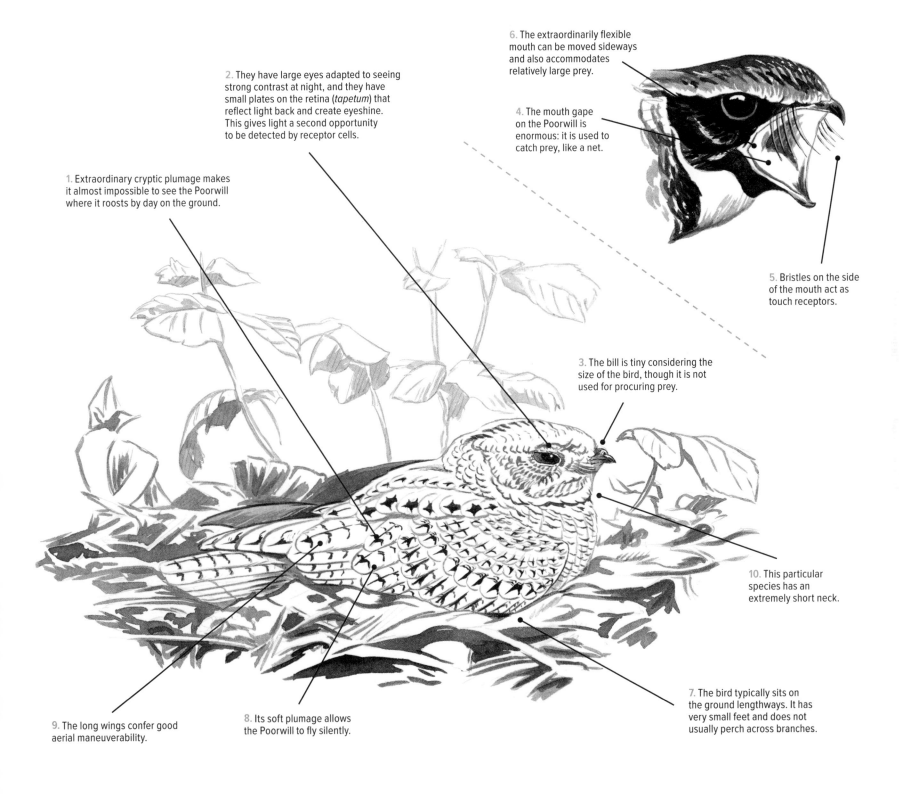

6. The extraordinarily flexible mouth can be moved sideways and also accommodates relatively large prey.

4. The mouth gape on the Poorwill is enormous: it is used to catch prey, like a net.

5. Bristles on the side of the mouth act as touch receptors.

2. They have large eyes adapted to seeing strong contrast at night, and they have small plates on the retina (*tapetum*) that reflect light back and create eyeshine. This gives light a second opportunity to be detected by receptor cells.

1. Extraordinary cryptic plumage makes it almost impossible to see the Poorwill where it roosts by day on the ground.

3. The bill is tiny considering the size of the bird, though it is not used for procuring prey.

10. This particular species has an extremely short neck.

9. The long wings confer good aerial maneuverability.

8. Its soft plumage allows the Poorwill to fly silently.

7. The bird typically sits on the ground lengthways. It has very small feet and does not usually perch across branches.

Greater Roadrunner | *Geococcyx californianus*

Found year-round in parts of California, Nevada, Utah, Arizona, New Mexico, Colorado, Kansas, Missouri, Arkansas, Louisiana, and Texas.

IT IS PROBABLY A LITTLE UNFORTUNATE THAT THE ROADRUNNER is better known as the star of the 1949 cartoon series than as a real bird. For the actual Roadrunner is indeed one of our most perfectly adapted desert species with a fascinating and unusual lifestyle. It occurs in the southern United States, from California to Texas and all the way to Louisiana in the east, inhabiting arid and semi-arid areas with low scrub.

The name is entirely apt, because the Roadrunner is a terrestrial bird that seldom flies. It is capable of running at almost 20 mph (30 km/h) for sustained periods of time, either to escape from predators or to chase after prey. Its diet includes a wide range of foods, including insects, spiders, reptiles, and small mammals, which are caught in the bill and often beaten on a hard surface to kill them. Its most famous prey is the rattlesnake, which it catches by the head, using its strong and fast legs to dodge a potential bite.

These birds live in the desert, where it can be cold at night. In the morning, they allow the sun to warm the skin on their back by ruffling their feathers, while during the hours of darkness they can reduce their core body temperature to save energy.

DID YOU KNOW?

Roadrunners will sometimes eat their own young when food is short.

10 THINGS TO REMEMBER

1. The long tail acts as balance when the bird is running and also as a rudder at full speed. Its tail is usually cocked, but lowered when running fast.

2. Strong legs with lengthened bones are an adaptation to terrestrial (on the ground) life.

3. This bird has an unusual foot arrangement—two toes face forward and two backward. The toes are lengthened for running on a flat surface.

4. Its wings are small, but the Roadrunner can fly when necessary.

5. The strong, hooked bill is ideal for dealing with live, and often quite dangerous, prey.

6. Back feathers can be fluffed up, letting the sun soak through to the skin. The skin is heavily pigmented with melanin, a substance that absorbs sunlight, warming the bird up.

7. The Roadrunner has cryptic plumage for concealment.

8. The orange markings behind the eye are shown in threat display.

9. The crest is raised in various social situations.

10. Lizards are a common prey, along with snakes, scorpions, tarantulas, and other desert animals.

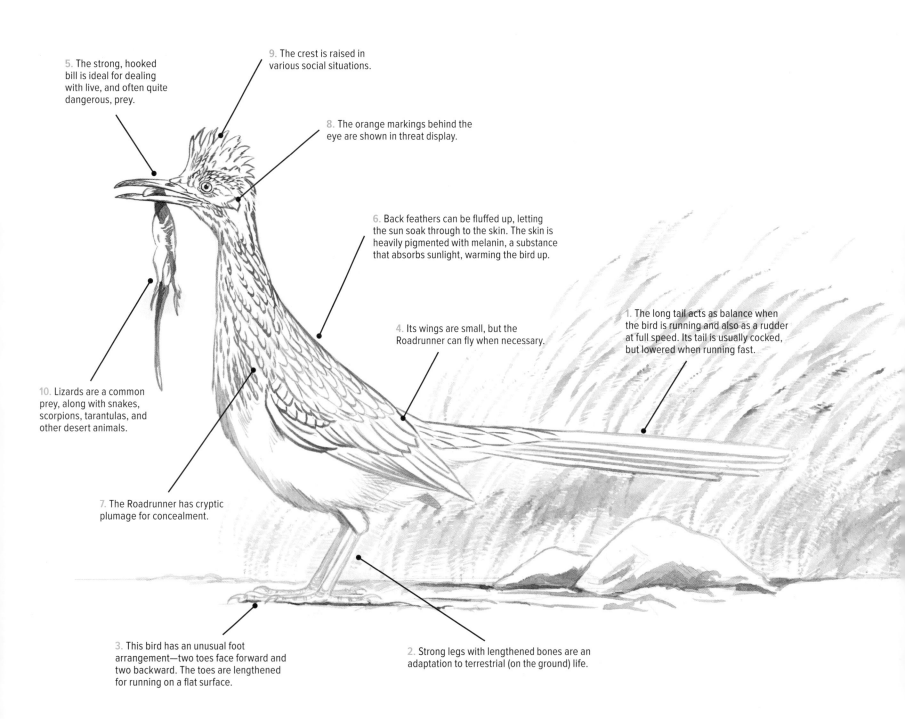

5. The strong, hooked bill is ideal for dealing with live, and often quite dangerous, prey.

9. The crest is raised in various social situations.

8. The orange markings behind the eye are shown in threat display.

6. Back feathers can be fluffed up, letting the sun soak through to the skin. The skin is heavily pigmented with melanin, a substance that absorbs sunlight, warming the bird up.

4. Its wings are small, but the Roadrunner can fly when necessary.

1. The long tail acts as balance when the bird is running and also as a rudder at full speed. Its tail is usually cocked, but lowered when running fast.

10. Lizards are a common prey, along with snakes, scorpions, tarantulas, and other desert animals.

7. The Roadrunner has cryptic plumage for concealment.

3. This bird has an unusual foot arrangement—two toes face forward and two backward. The toes are lengthened for running on a flat surface.

2. Strong legs with lengthened bones are an adaptation to terrestrial (on the ground) life.

Ruby-throated Hummingbird | *Archilochus colubris*

Summers mainly east of the Great Plains, from Ontario, Quebec, and Nova Scotia, and south to Florida and the Gulf Coast. It also reaches northwest of the Plains to Alberta, Saskatchewan, and Manitoba. Winters in Mexico.

FOR MANY AMERICANS, THIS IS THE ONLY HUMMINGBIRD SPECIES they have ever seen. Despite a healthy number of species in the West, and even more in the Arizona border region, the Ruby-throated Hummingbird is the only species of its family inhabiting much of the eastern side of our continent. It is a summer visitor, occurring in woodland areas and frequently visiting gardens to drink at blooms and at hummingbird feeders.

Among the most celebrated of all birds, Hummers acquire much of their nutriment by hovering at flowers and drinking nectar. In order to do this, they must flap their wings approximately 80 times a second; the wings follow a unique path that resembles a figure eight, and this provides astonishing maneuverability and, at times, great speed—some hummers can fly at 62 mph (100 km/h). It will come as a surprise to many people that Hummingbirds also eat a lot of insects and spiders, picking these up all the time as they hunt around flowers. They provide the birds with important extra protein.

The Ruby-throated Hummingbird is famous for its proven ability to migrate considerable distances. Some fly across the Gulf of Mexico—at distances further than 1,242 miles (2,000 km)—in a single hop. In preparation, they almost double their own body weight—from not much to slightly more!

10 THINGS TO REMEMBER

1. The Ruby-throated Hummingbird is miniature in size—only 3 ½ inches (9 cm) long and weighs 0.1 ounces (3.5 g).

2. [Inset] The long bill allows it to reach into flowers to drink nectar.

3. [Inset] The bill contains a long tongue which is fitted with tiny grooves that lead to the mouth. Fluids pass up these grooves by a force called "capillary action," so the Hummingbird does not need to suck.

4. Tiny feet with long claws allow it to perch, but it cannot walk or hop.

5. [Inset] The bright red area on the throat is called the "gorget" and is found on the male only. The iridescence is purely a function of light refraction—the feather pigments are actually brown.

6. Hummingbirds have the fewest feathers of any family of birds.

7. Hovering is the main feeding method.

8. The wings move in a unique figure-eight pattern while the bird is hovering, allowing the forward and backward movement—a Hummer can even fly upside down briefly.

9. The Ruby-throated Hummingbird has spiky tail feathers. These make a whistling sound when the bird dives through the air in display, adding sound to the visual effect.

10. Red flowers are especially popular with this species.

2. The long bill allows it to reach into flowers to drink nectar.

3. The bill contains a long tongue which is fitted with tiny grooves that lead to the mouth. Fluids pass up these grooves by a force called "capillary action," so the Hummingbird does not need to suck.

5. The bright red area on the throat is called the "gorget" and is found on the male only. The iridescence is purely a function of light refraction—the feather pigments are actually brown.

1. The Ruby-throated Hummingbird is miniature in size—only 3 ½ inches (9 cm) long and weighs 0.1 ounces (3.5 g).

8. The wings move in a unique figure-eight pattern while the bird is hovering, allowing the forward and backward movement—a Hummer can even fly upside down briefly.

4. Tiny feet with long claws allow it to perch, but it cannot walk or hop.

7. Hovering is the main feeding method.

10. Red flowers are especially popular with this species.

9. The Ruby-throated Hummingbird has spiky tail feathers. These make a whistling sound when the bird dives through the air in display, adding sound to the visual effect.

6. Hummingbirds have the fewest feathers of any family of birds.

Belted Kingfisher | *Megaceryle alcyon*

Breeds throughout North America except for Arctic Canada. Mainly a summer visitor north of the Great Lakes, and it is mainly a winter visitor to the very southern United States.

WITH ITS LOUD, RATTLING CALL, THE BELTED KINGFISHER is usually heard before it is seen. But once in view, it is a large and unmistakable bird. It is one of North America's most widely distributed species, occurring almost throughout the whole continent. North of the Great Lakes, though, it is mainly a summer visitor.

As its name implies, the Belted Kingfisher is mainly a consumer of fish, although it will also take some aquatic invertebrates such as crayfish. It catches these food items through a modified version of the "perch-and-pounce" system, seen in many predatory birds. It sits on an elevated perch, watching below for movement. Once it has spotted something, it dives down. In the Kingfisher's version, this involves a head-first plunge and dexterous grab with its bill. Catching fish from above isn't easy —the fish can easily get spooked, and the hunter has to compensate for refraction—but somehow the Belted Kingfisher finds enough to survive.

For breeding, these birds dig out a burrow in a muddy or sandy bank, which may be as long as 6½ feet (2 m). In a chamber at the end, the female lays white eggs and incubates them for about 3 weeks.

10 THINGS TO REMEMBER

1. The Belted Kingfisher typically sits on an elevated perch above the water, where it watches for the movement of fish below.

2. The long, straight, daggerlike bill is typical of a fish-eating bird.

3. The bill is laterally compressed, giving it a knifelike shape, so it moves through the water with little resistance when the bird dives in.

4. The bird has small legs, in which the three toes pointing forward are partially joined. This might help the Kingfisher dig out its nest hole.

5. The dark feathering around the eyes probably helps to reduce glare.

6. Kingfishers angle their heads down when they have caught sight of something. This helps them to judge distance to their prey. When the head is horizontal, they can see further around them but not as accurately.

7. Long but broad wings enable it to fly slow and low over the water, and to hover at times.

8. Shaggy crest breaks up the line of its head.

9. Sexes are distinguished by breast coloration. Female (as shown here) has a chestnut band across her chest, while the male has a gray band.

10. Pale eyespots are raised when the Kingfisher is threatened.

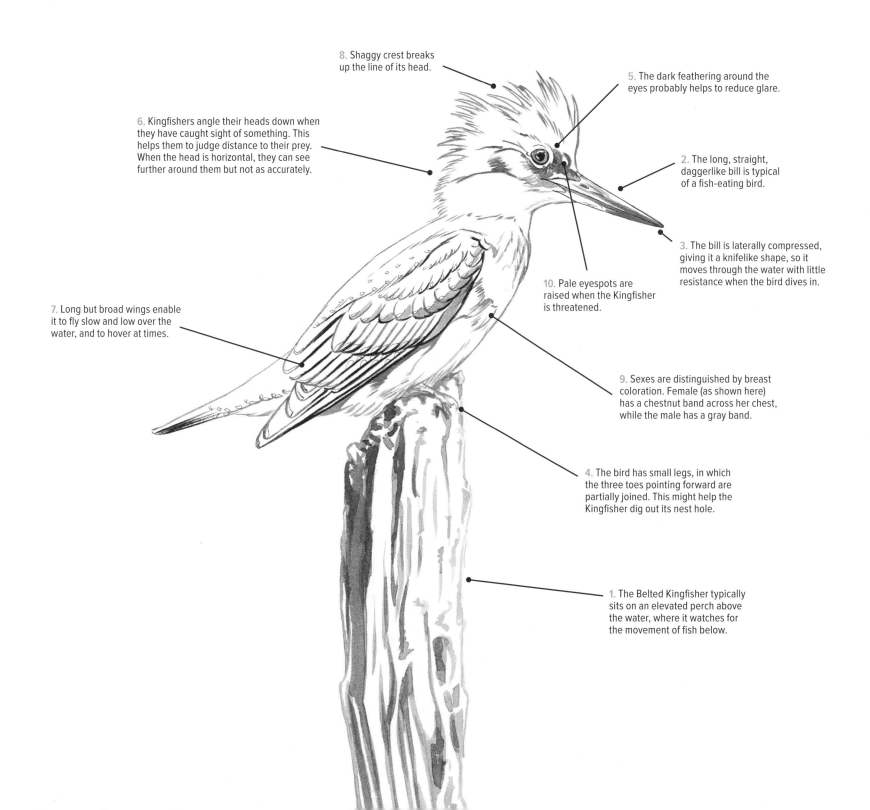

8. Shaggy crest breaks up the line of its head.

5. The dark feathering around the eyes probably helps to reduce glare.

6. Kingfishers angle their heads down when they have caught sight of something. This helps them to judge distance to their prey. When the head is horizontal, they can see further around them but not as accurately.

2. The long, straight, daggerlike bill is typical of a fish-eating bird.

3. The bill is laterally compressed, giving it a knifelike shape, so it moves through the water with little resistance when the bird dives in.

10. Pale eyespots are raised when the Kingfisher is threatened.

7. Long but broad wings enable it to fly slow and low over the water, and to hover at times.

9. Sexes are distinguished by breast coloration. Female (as shown here) has a chestnut band across her chest, while the male has a gray band.

4. The bird has small legs, in which the three toes pointing forward are partially joined. This might help the Kingfisher dig out its nest hole.

1. The Belted Kingfisher typically sits on an elevated perch above the water, where it watches for the movement of fish below.

Acorn Woodpecker | *Melanerpes formicivorus*

Found year-round in parts of Oregon, California, Arizona, New Mexico, and Texas.

IN SOME WAYS THE ACORN WOODPECKER is very typical of the woodpecker species, and in other ways it is highly unusual. It is a common and conspicuous bird of the oak-dominated woodlands of the Southwest.

The Acorn Woodpecker is certainly shaped like a typical woodpecker, with its chisel-shaped bill, stiff tail, and strong legs, and it is usually seen holding onto the vertical stems of trees. Equally it can use its bill to bore holes and, like other woodpeckers, it has a varied diet of insects (including ants) and plant material.

What is abnormal about the Acorn Woodpecker, however, is its habit of living in small groups of up to four males and three females which together defend large stores of acorns and other seeds. The birds select a suitable site, either in a tree or—as often happens—in a utility pole, and there they make thousands of small holes into which they lodge the fruits available to them in the fall for later consumption. These "granaries" are known to have as many as 50,000 holes.

The groups live together year-round and when it comes to breeding, every bird takes part in feeding the young.

10 THINGS TO REMEMBER

1. The typical woodpecker posture that is illustrated on the opposite page is clinging onto a vertical tree trunk.

2. Strong, long, pointed bill is ideal for making holes in trees.

3. [Inset] Unusual arrangement of toes, with two facing forward and two backward ("zygodactyl") helps the woodpecker to keep good balance on trees.

4. [Inset] Long, sharp claws give better grip.

5. Tail has specially stiffened feathers, which take the weight of the woodpecker when it is on a vertical limb.

6. Many species of woodpeckers have bright red markings on the crown.

7. Typical black-and-white plumage makes the woodpecker difficult to see when in tree branches, especially when viewed against the sky.

8. The typical food of this species is acorns, which are both long-lasting and nutritious.

9. This species spends much time drilling holes in trees (and telephone poles) and lodging acorns that it has collected inside them. Small groups defend the stores ("granaries") they have collected and live cooperatively.

10. White staring eye on clownlike face. These probably help in species, or even individual recognition.

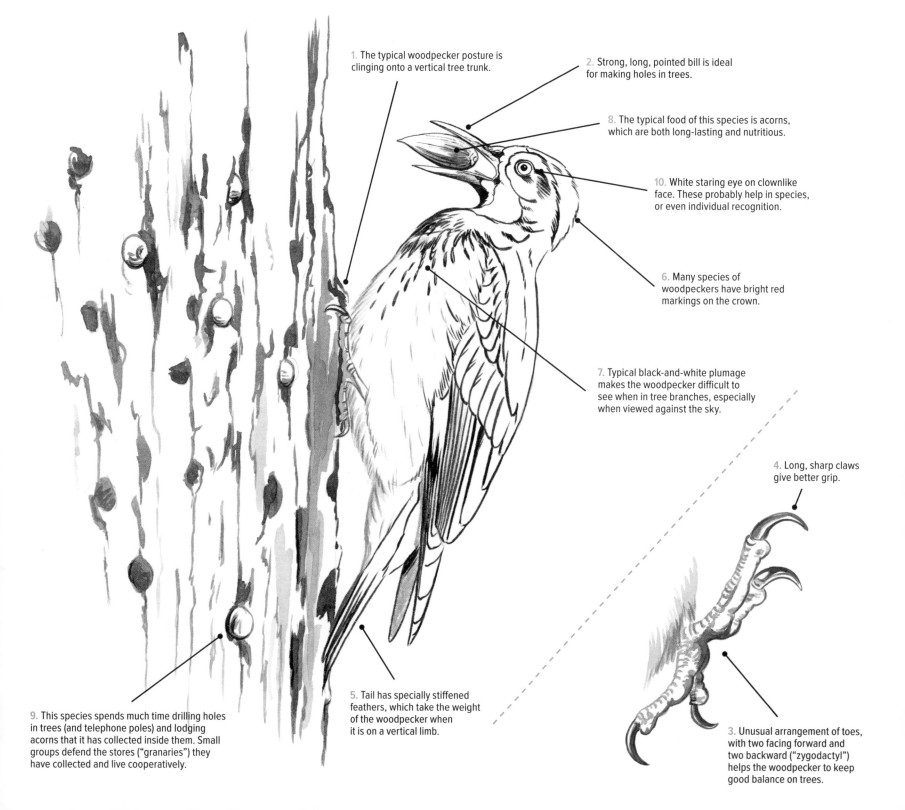

1. The typical woodpecker posture is clinging onto a vertical tree trunk.

2. Strong, long, pointed bill is ideal for making holes in trees.

8. The typical food of this species is acorns, which are both long-lasting and nutritious.

10. White staring eye on clownlike face. These probably help in species, or even individual recognition.

6. Many species of woodpeckers have bright red markings on the crown.

7. Typical black-and-white plumage makes the woodpecker difficult to see when in tree branches, especially when viewed against the sky.

4. Long, sharp claws give better grip.

5. Tail has specially stiffened feathers, which take the weight of the woodpecker when it is on a vertical limb.

9. This species spends much time drilling holes in trees (and telephone poles) and lodging acorns that it has collected inside them. Small groups defend the stores ("granaries") they have collected and live cooperatively.

3. Unusual arrangement of toes, with two facing forward and two backward ("zygodactyl") helps the woodpecker to keep good balance on trees.

Northern Flicker | *Colaptes auratus*

Breeds throughout North America south of the tree line. Mainly a summer visitor to Canada. Found in much of Texas and Southern California, but only in the winter.

THE NORTHERN FLICKER, ALTHOUGH SHAPED LIKE SIMILAR WOODPECKERS, feeds mainly on the ground in the open, and often far from cover. Other woodpeckers are usually confined to trees. The Northern Flicker does not make holes in trees for feeding, but instead strikes the ground to dislodge earth and expose ants and other insects.

Flickers feed primarily on ants, and they may spend minutes on end working at a single anthill. They lap the insects up with their long tongue, just like anteaters. Their remarkable tongues project up to 1.5 inches (4 cm) beyond the bill; the tip is capable of moving independently, and the whole tongue is coated with sticky saliva from the bird's large glands, which means that the ants simply stick to the surface and are easily ingested.

Northern Flickers do use their bills for excavation, but they predominantly use them to build nesting and roosting sites. A pair usually selects a dead tree on which to work, but may occasionally use a burrow in the ground. Both sexes excavate the cavity and the female lays 5–8 white eggs, which both birds take turns to incubate.

The Northern Flicker exhibits considerable color variation across the wide area of North America they inhabit. Eastern birds have yellow under the wing, and a black moustache; western birds are salmon-pink under the wing, and have a red moustache.

10 THINGS TO REMEMBER

1. Large black mark on breast acts as disruptive camouflage by breaking up the shape of the bird from a distance, making it less obvious to predators.

2. In contrast to most other woodpecker species, the Northern Flicker feeds chiefly on the ground rather than in the trees, looking for ants.

3. Stripe running from bill is black on eastern birds and red on western individuals.

4. Has long bill typical of a woodpecker, but in this species it is slightly curved, adapted for probing rather than drilling.

5. Brown back affords camouflage when bird is hunting on the ground.

6. [Inset] Long tongue enables bird to lap up ants easily. It protrudes 1.5 inches (4 cm) beyond the tip of the bill.

7. [Inset] Tip of tongue is capable of independent movement and can probe into bark fissures and ant burrows.

8. Stiff tail shows that Northern Flickers are as capable as other woodpeckers of clinging vertically to trees.

9. Strong legs and feet.

10. Rounded wings allow for strong flight in confined spaces. Like all woodpeckers, flickers fly with strongly undulating ("bounding") flight, with bursts of flaps interspersed with the wings held in.

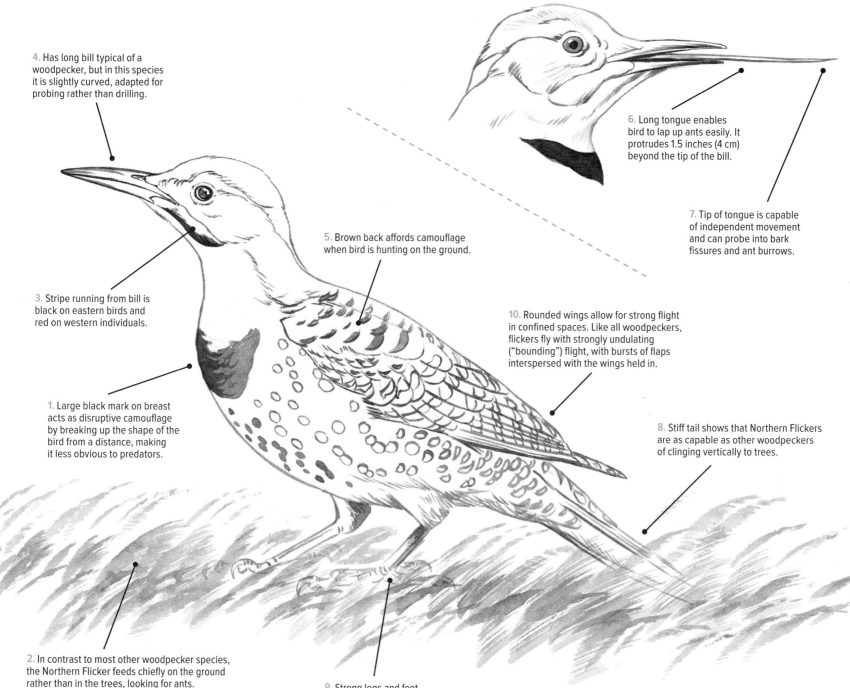

4. Has long bill typical of a woodpecker, but in this species it is slightly curved, adapted for probing rather than drilling.

6. Long tongue enables bird to lap up ants easily. It protrudes 1.5 inches (4 cm) beyond the tip of the bill.

7. Tip of tongue is capable of independent movement and can probe into bark fissures and ant burrows.

3. Stripe running from bill is black on eastern birds and red on western individuals.

5. Brown back affords camouflage when bird is hunting on the ground.

10. Rounded wings allow for strong flight in confined spaces. Like all woodpeckers, flickers fly with strongly undulating ("bounding") flight, with bursts of flaps interspersed with the wings held in.

1. Large black mark on breast acts as disruptive camouflage by breaking up the shape of the bird from a distance, making it less obvious to predators.

8. Stiff tail shows that Northern Flickers are as capable as other woodpeckers of clinging vertically to trees.

2. In contrast to most other woodpecker species, the Northern Flicker feeds chiefly on the ground rather than in the trees, looking for ants.

9. Strong legs and feet.

Western Kingbird | *Tyrannus verticalis*

Breeds mainly west of the Mississippi, from the Canadian border southward. Winters in Mexico and Florida.

THE WESTERN KINGBIRD IS ONE OF SEVERAL VERY SIMILAR SPECIES of Kingbird that are found in the Southwest. They are inhabitants of open country and are routinely observed perching on posts and overhead wires. It is common to see them during car journeys alongside country roads. They are members of the so-called Tyrant Flycatcher family (*Tyrannidae*), a family that is known for being both extremely aggressive, mobbing passing hawks and other intruders without the slightest hesitation, and also being particularly skilled in the art of catching flies when airborne. Their primary feeding method involves keeping watch from an elevated perch, flying out toward their prey, and then snapping up their catch in their bill, often audibly. They can also snatch prey from the ground and will also prey on shrubs to pluck berries.

Male Western Kingbirds undertake showy displays in the spring, when they fly up and down in front of a watching female, taking a zigzag path and uttering a soft, spluttering call. They also sing a "Dawn Song," beginning and ending so early in the morning that it is still dark. The nest, built by both sexes, is made up of a cup of grass and other soft materials placed in the fork of a tree, or sometimes on the ledge of a building. Prior to choosing the site, the male performs a "nest-showing" routine to the female, which basically consists of perching at a suitable site and lowering its belly down, as if it were incubating eggs.

10 THINGS TO REMEMBER

1. Large flying insects are the Kingbird's main prey, including bees, beetles, crickets, katydids, and butterflies.

2. Prey is usually caught during flight but Western Kingbirds will also glean prey from foliage and consume their catch on the ground.

3. All prey is caught individually, rather than the hunter simply flying through the air with his mouth open, hoping to catch an insect.

4. Has long, broad wings—typical of a bird that requires agile flight with many twists and turns.

5. "Primary" feathers form the wing tip. The male Western Kingbird has extended primary tips, thought to be for use in spectacular flight display.

6. "Secondary" feathers form inner trailing edge of wing. The edge needs to be thin and even, allowing for an orderly flow of air.

7. "Coverts" cover and protect the bases of the main flight feathers, the primaries and secondaries.

8. In common with many birds, the Kingbird has white outer tail feathers which make the bird more conspicuous to other species. White feathers may also be more resistant to wear.

9. [Inset] The bill is extremely broad-based to give the bird a greater reach when catching prey.

10. [Inset] There are small bristles at base of bill. These have a sense of touch, helping the bird to detect prey that is close to the mouth.

1. Large flying insects are the Kingbird's main prey, including bees, beetles, crickets, katydids, and butterflies.

2. Prey is usually caught during flight but Western Kingbirds will also glean prey from foliage and consume their catch on the ground.

3. All prey is caught individually, rather than the hunter simply flying through the air with his mouth open, hoping to catch an insect.

4. Has long, broad wings—typical of a bird that requires agile flight with many twists and turns.

5. "Primary" feathers form the wing tip. The male Western Kingbird has extended primary tips, thought to be for use in spectacular flight display.

6. "Secondary" feathers form inner trailing edge of wing. The edge needs to be thin and even, allowing for an orderly flow of air.

7. "Coverts" cover and protect the bases of the main flight feathers, the primaries and secondaries.

8. In common with many birds, the Kingbird has white outer tail feathers which make the bird more conspicuous to other species. White feathers may also be more resistant to wear.

9. The bill is extremely broad-based to give the bird a greater reach when catching prey.

10. There are small bristles at base of bill. These have a sense of touch, helping the bird to detect prey that is close to the mouth.

Red-eyed Vireo | *Vireo olivaceus*

Breeds throughout the eastern half of North America and north to northern Ontario, Quebec, the Maritime Provinces, and southern Newfoundland. In the western half, breeds in British Columbia, the Northwest Territories, Alberta, and Saskatchewan to states south of the Canadian border, including Washington, Oregon, Idaho, and Montana. Winters in South America.

SOME SCIENTISTS CLAIM THAT THE RED-EYED VIREO is one of the most common species of birds in the deciduous woodlands of eastern North America, however it has managed to keep a low profile and many members of the public have never heard of it. That could be for a number of reasons—it is a plain-colored bird and tends to reside in the canopy and sub-canopy of forests. The Red-eyed Vireo does not share people's gardens with other birds.

Vireos are small birds and when grouped together may be mistaken for warblers. However, they lack the bright coloring of warblers, and in comparison to their frenetic colleagues, they move in a slow, deliberate manner. They do, however, share similar food tastes and in the summer, Red-eyed Vireos subsist almost entirely upon caterpillars gleaned from leaves. In the fall, the diet switches and Vireos consume many seeds and berries.

The song of the Red-eyed Vireo is a monotonous repetitive refrain that has been transcribed as *"Here I am, where are you? Here I am, where are you?"* repetitively, sometimes for hours on end. Males are highly territorial and spend hours sticking close to their mates to prevent them from copulating with nearby rivals. The nest is an intricately woven cup suspended from a tree fork.

DID YOU KNOW?

An adult male Red-eyed Vireo was once heard to sing 22,197 times in a single 14-hour day!

10 THINGS TO REMEMBER

1. Vireos have green colored backs. The family name "Vireo" literally means "to be green."

2. Long, pointed wings aid the bird's flight and extended migration. The Vireo flies to the Amazon Basin in the winter.

3. The feathers making up the wing tip are called the "primaries." A Vireo has nine of these, the same number as other small birds.

4. Fairly short tail. This can be raised and fanned in threat display.

5. Mainly dull coloration for moving around inconspicuously.

6. [Inset] Fairly thick bill with a hook at the tip, which helps to keep hold of live insects. There are also two tiny notches near the tip of the upper portion of the bill, which almost certainly do the same thing inside the bill.

7. [Inset] Red coloring of eye. The intensity varies between adults and depends on the individual. Juveniles have black eyes.

8. [Inset] Black stripe covers the eye.

9. Crown can be raised when bird is agitated.

10. Vireos are not agile birds and do not often hover or assume acrobatic postures (as warblers do).

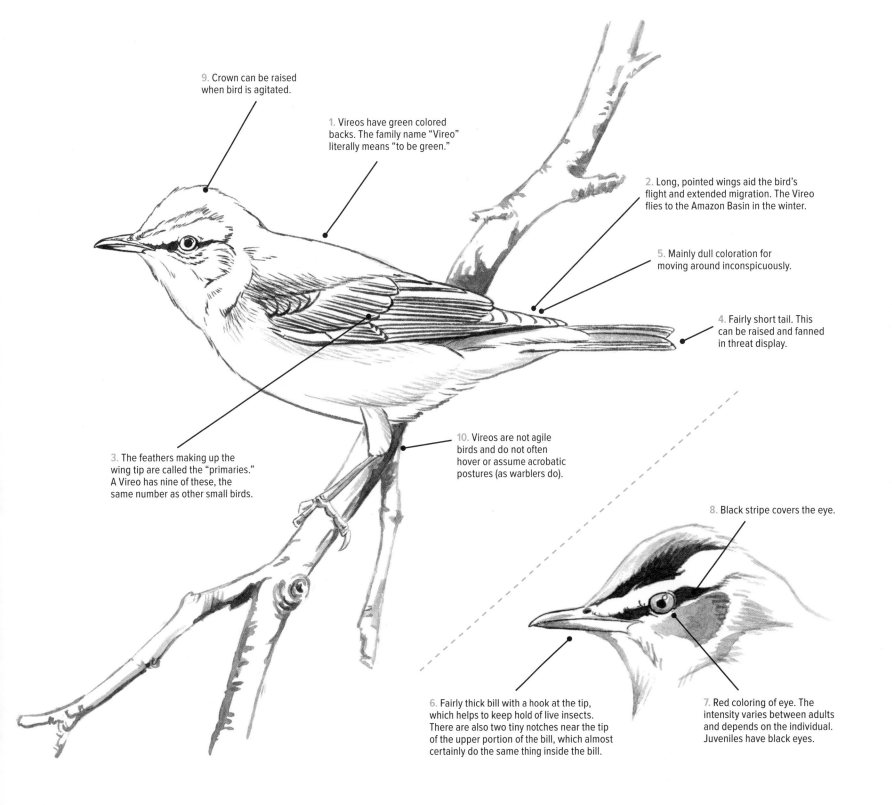

9. Crown can be raised when bird is agitated.

1. Vireos have green colored backs. The family name "Vireo" literally means "to be green."

2. Long, pointed wings aid the bird's flight and extended migration. The Vireo flies to the Amazon Basin in the winter.

5. Mainly dull coloration for moving around inconspicuously.

4. Fairly short tail. This can be raised and fanned in threat display.

3. The feathers making up the wing tip are called the "primaries." A Vireo has nine of these, the same number as other small birds.

10. Vireos are not agile birds and do not often hover or assume acrobatic postures (as warblers do).

8. Black stripe covers the eye.

6. Fairly thick bill with a hook at the tip, which helps to keep hold of live insects. There are also two tiny notches near the tip of the upper portion of the bill, which almost certainly do the same thing inside the bill.

7. Red coloring of eye. The intensity varies between adults and depends on the individual. Juveniles have black eyes.

Violet-green Swallow | *Tachycineta thalassina*

Very much a western bird, breeding from Central Alaska and western Canada down to the Mexican border, covering all western states east to North and South Dakota, Nebraska, Montana, Colorado, and Texas. Winters from California to Central America.

THERE ARE PLENTY OF GAUDILY COLORFUL BIRDS IN NORTH AMERICA, but few are as tastefully hued as the exquisite Violet-green Swallow of the mountainous west. It is aptly named, with iridescent green and violet on the wings and rump respectively, together with a green crown and predominantly white face.

In common with every member of the Swallow and Martin family, Violet-green Swallows are aerial birds, spending much of their time in flight catching insects such as flies, aphids, and winged ants. It is thought that they catch these small prey individually, rather than simply trawling through the skies with bills wide open. Compared to most other Swallow species, Violet-greens tend to fly higher in the air and take smaller prey.

Swallow species either construct nests of mud, or build their nests in an existing cavity. The Violet-green Swallow selects a tree hole for its cup-shaped nest, which it builds of straw and lines with feathers. Pairs sometimes nest in isolation, but dead trees frequently offer several cavities, allowing colonies to form in a single tree. The Violet-green Swallow is chiefly found in these woodland areas because of the need for empty tree holes to nest in.

10 THINGS TO REMEMBER

1. Long, sharply pointed wings give exceptional flying skill and mobility.

2. Tail is slightly forked, to allow further maneuverability for catching insects in flight.

3. Often glides in flight. Other species, such as the Barn Swallow, glide less frequently.

4. Stunning green and violet coloration on back.

5. White patches on sides of rump may help species recognition, or allow birds to keep in visual contact with one another.

6. [Inset] Small feet allow for perching, but majority of time is spent in the air.

7. Slim, streamlined body for efficient flight.

8. [Inset] Swallows have small, short bills, but very wide gapes for catching flying insects.

9. The Swallow builds its nest inside tree cavities.

10. White coloring and distinctive markings on the face enable the different species of swallows to recognize each other.

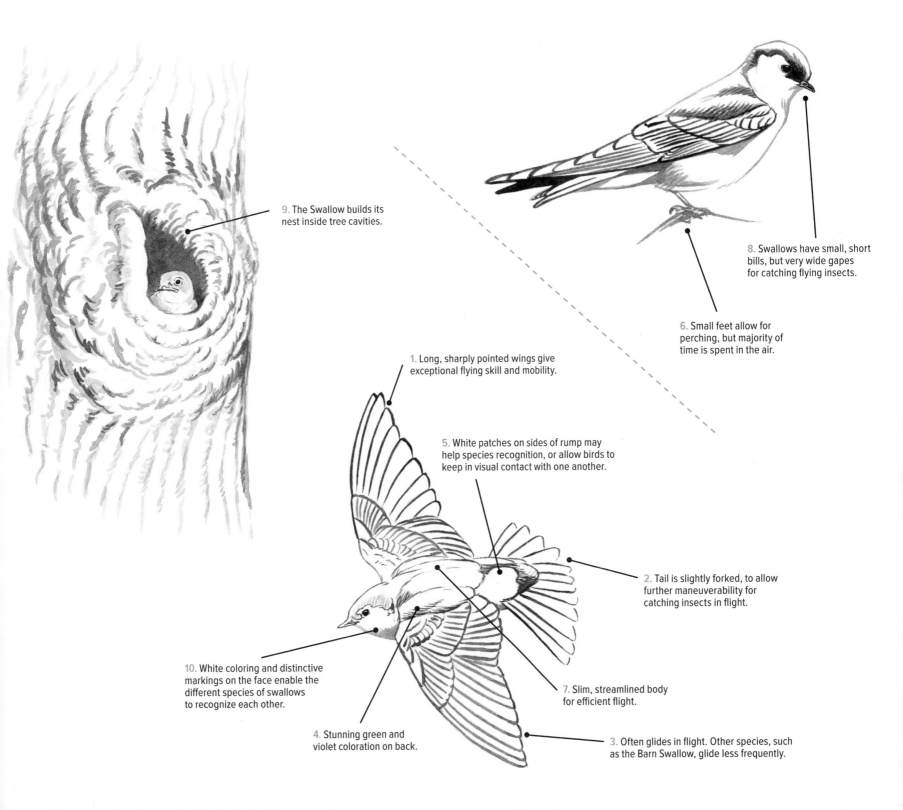

9. The Swallow builds its nest inside tree cavities.

8. Swallows have small, short bills, but very wide gapes for catching flying insects.

6. Small feet allow for perching, but majority of time is spent in the air.

1. Long, sharply pointed wings give exceptional flying skill and mobility.

5. White patches on sides of rump may help species recognition, or allow birds to keep in visual contact with one another.

2. Tail is slightly forked, to allow further maneuverability for catching insects in flight.

10. White coloring and distinctive markings on the face enable the different species of swallows to recognize each other.

7. Slim, streamlined body for efficient flight.

4. Stunning green and violet coloration on back.

3. Often glides in flight. Other species, such as the Barn Swallow, glide less frequently.

Golden-crowned Kinglet | *Regulus satrapa*

A bird of northern and mountain conifer forests, occurring from Alaska eastward to the Maritime Provinces and Newfoundland, south to the Appalachians and Rockies. Winters over much of the rest of North America.

THE SMALLEST BIRDS IN NORTH AMERICA (BAR HUMMINGBIRDS) are the kinglets, of which there are two species, Golden-crowned and Ruby-crowned. They are named "kinglets" after their crowns, which are brightly colored and are raised when the birds are excited or annoyed. Despite their size, Kinglets are often fearless toward people and aggressive to each other. They are also extremely fidgety, constantly flicking their wings, and moving from branch to branch at speed.

The Golden-crowned Kinglet is a bird of coniferous forests, both in the northern Boreal zone and in mountains. It inhabits the niche of gleaning very small insects from the needles and bark of conifers, especially spruces, sometimes hovering in hummingbirdlike fashion to reach a hard-to-get at food item. Few other birds feed in this habitat, so the Kinglets have relatively little competition.

Remarkably, Golden-crowned Kinglets are often resident in the northern forests, managing to cope with freezing overnight temperatures during the winter months. In order to survive cold nights they huddle together in bodily contact with others of their species. During the day, they are often found in mixed flocks with other species, each bird keeping a lookout for predators.

Kinglets build well-concealed nests deep within the thick branches of conifers, often using spiders' webs as part of the structure. They lay large clutches of 9–11 eggs and often have several broods a year, to compensate for high mortality.

10 THINGS TO REMEMBER

1. Tiny size is exceptional—one of the smallest North American birds.
2. Kinglets are found in conifers, especially spruce.
3. Exceptionally thin and weak bill is ideal for picking insects from conifer needles.
4. Needles form an unusual micro-habitat.
5. Thin legs are nevertheless strong and allow the bird to hang upside down when foraging.
6. Crown is yellow and orange in the male (only yellow in the female) and is often raised during interactions.
7. Bold crown stripes.
8. Wing bars are shown off when the bird flies, and it may indicate the presence of one individual to another.
9. Overall dull color is cryptic against background of foliage.
10. [Inset] Relatively short, rounded wings allow bird to maneuver in foliage, and even to hover.

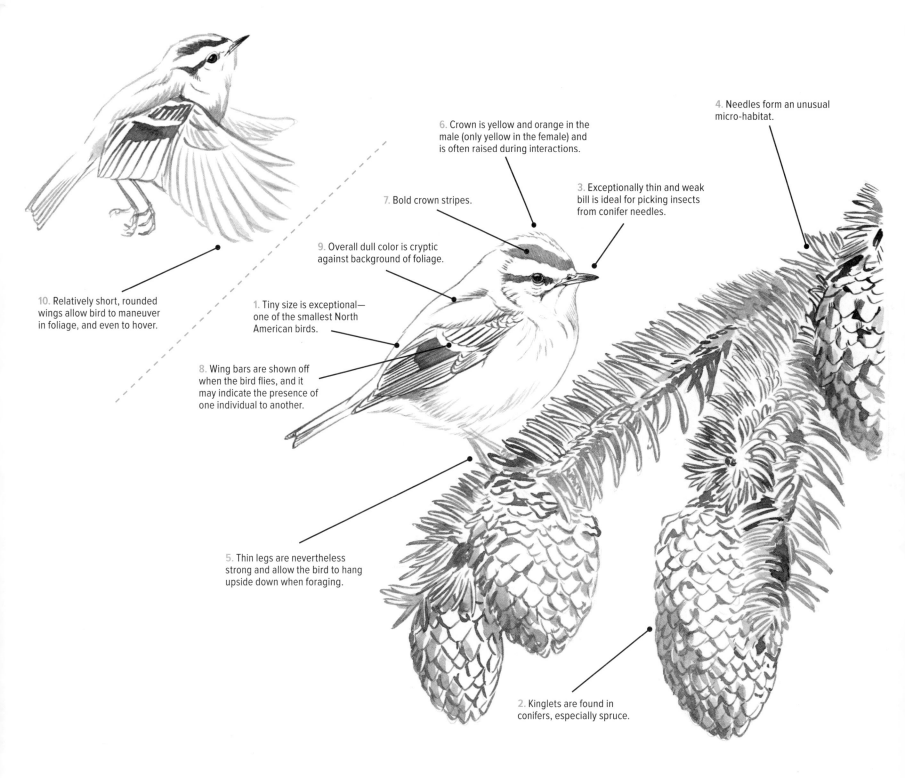

4. Needles form an unusual micro-habitat.

6. Crown is yellow and orange in the male (only yellow in the female) and is often raised during interactions.

3. Exceptionally thin and weak bill is ideal for picking insects from conifer needles.

7. Bold crown stripes.

9. Overall dull color is cryptic against background of foliage.

10. Relatively short, rounded wings allow bird to maneuver in foliage, and even to hover.

1. Tiny size is exceptional— one of the smallest North American birds.

8. Wing bars are shown off when the bird flies, and it may indicate the presence of one individual to another.

5. Thin legs are nevertheless strong and allow the bird to hang upside down when foraging.

2. Kinglets are found in conifers, especially spruce.

Cape May Warbler | *Dendroica tigrina*

Breeds in a narrow band of taiga forest from the Northwest Territories and south Alberta and east across Saskatchewan, Manitoba, Minnesota, Wisconsin, Michigan, New York, Vermont, New Hampshire, Maine, Ontario, Quebec, and the Maritime Provinces. Winters on islands in the Caribbean.

NOBODY COULD MISTAKE THE BRILLIANTLY COLORED MALE Cape May Warbler for another bird in the springtime. In the fall, however, the bird's modest appearance can make it difficult to find among flocks of warblers that have similarly changed their plumage. Unmistakable and handsome in the breeding season when it needs to impress a mate, the Cape May Warbler is dowdy and more cryptic during the fall and winter, when its focus is on survival alone.

This attractive bird doesn't only swap its plumage from season to season, but has a similarly dramatic change in lifestyle during the year. In the spring, it lives in the Boreal forest zone, spending much of its time foraging for insects among spruces, gleaning from the needles, and even hovering in front of treetop branches. During this season it has a particular penchant for a caterpillar called the Spruce Budworm, which often occurs in large infestations and is a major constituent of the summer diet. In the fall, however, the Cape May Warbler undertakes a long-distance migration to the islands of the West Indies. Here it feeds not just on insects, but also on nectar, using its semi-tubular tongue to feed. No other relative bird has such a tongue.

10 THINGS TO REMEMBER

1. [Top] Bright colors of breeding plumage. New feathers on body are grown in late winter.
2. [Top] Wing feathers on this bird are retained from the fall.
3. [Bottom] The nonbreeding plumage displayed here is much less colorful than breeding plumage. These feathers are grown in July.
4. [Bottom] Wing feathers grown in late summer will be kept for one year.
5. [Top] Bright red cheeks shown off in display.
6. White spots on tail may help birds to see each other in flocks.
7. The long, pointed wings are typical of a landbird that makes a long-distance migration.
8. The thin bill is typical of insectivorous birds that glean foliage.
9. Slight curve of bill may be an adaptation to feeding on nectar in nonbreeding season.
10. Foot typical of perching bird—three toes point forward, one behind.

COLOR YOURSELF **SMART** INSECT-EATING BIRDS
BIRDS OF NORTH AMERICA

Top – Breeding plumage
Bottom – Nonbreeding plumage

2. Wing feathers on this bird are retained from the fall.

8. The thin bill is typical of insectivorous birds that glean foliage.

5. Bright red cheeks shown off in display.

6. White spots on tail may help birds to see each other in flocks.

1. Bright colors of breeding plumage. New feathers on body are grown in late winter.

4. Wing feathers grown in late summer will be kept for one year.

9. Slight curve of bill may be an adaptation to feeding on nectar in nonbreeding season.

3. The nonbreeding plumage displayed here is much less colorful than breeding plumage. These feathers are grown in July.

7. The long, pointed wings are typical of a landbird that makes a long-distance migration.

10. Foot typical of perching bird— three toes point forward, one behind.

Common Yellowthroat | *Geothlypis trichas*

Breeds throughout North America except for the desert regions of the Southwest. Present all year in California and in the Southeast. Many winter in Mexico.

THE COMMON YELLOWTHROAT IS A GOOD EXAMPLE of a bird that is far more often heard than seen. Its monotonous *"witchity-witchity-witchity"* song is a common sound in the summer, echoing from every small patch of wet brush or marshland right across the continent, yet the bird itself can be difficult to see. Indeed, the birds themselves rely greatly on sound to make clear their intentions to other birds.

The Yellowthroat is one of our most variable warblers, with different populations exhibiting differences in overall color brightness and in the width of the pale band between the mask and the crown. The size of bird also differs, with large individuals being found in the Southwest, for example, and small individuals along the Pacific coast. Altogether there are some 13 races of Yellowthroat, including those in Mexico.

As befits a bird that spends most of its time in low vegetation, the Yellowthroat builds its nest close to the ground, 3 feet (1 m) away at the very most. It is a bulky structure made from weeds and grass stems, and is cup-shaped with a partial, fragile roof. The female lays 3–5 eggs which hatch after 12 days and are fed by both parents.

10 THINGS TO REMEMBER

1. Black face mask is found only in the male.
2. The band between mask, crown, and nape varies—it is wider in birds from the Southwest.
3. Overall color varies regionally. Some birds are more yellow, others more brown.
4. The Common Yellowthroat has relatively short wings for a migratory bird (some populations don't travel very far).
5. Rounded wings allow the Yellowthroat to flit around in thick vegetation.
6. The thin bill is ideal for gleaning insects off foliage.
7. Usually holds onto perch as it grabs insect from leaf, but can also make short flights to snap up flying prey.
8. Throughout North America, thick vegetation close to the ground is the Yellowthroat's prime habitat. Habitats are often wet, such as marshes.
9. Tail often flicked by male in display.
10. Yellowthroats are very noisy, typical of birds living in thick underbrush that cannot easily see other members of their own species.

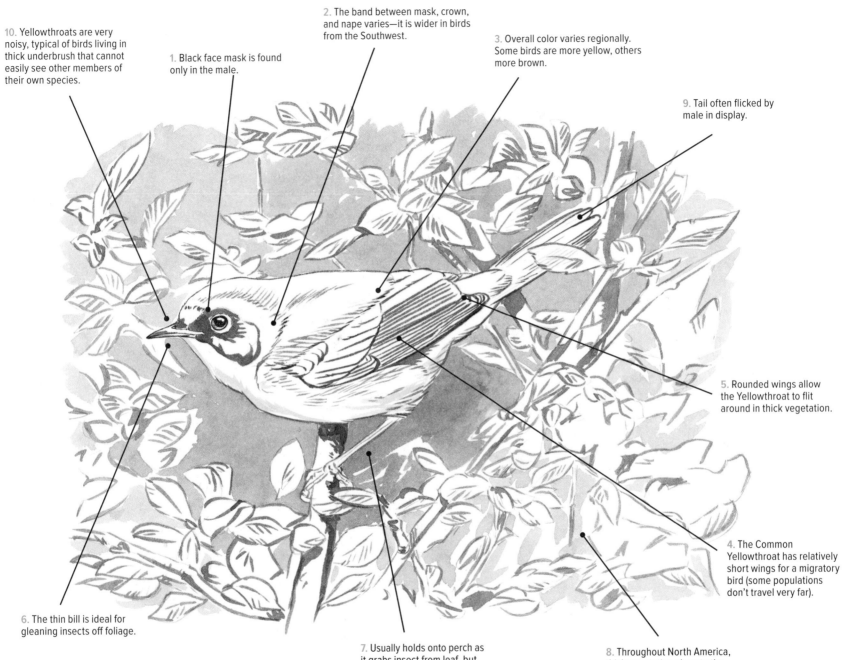

10. Yellowthroats are very noisy, typical of birds living in thick underbrush that cannot easily see other members of their own species.

1. Black face mask is found only in the male.

2. The band between mask, crown, and nape varies—it is wider in birds from the Southwest.

3. Overall color varies regionally. Some birds are more yellow, others more brown.

9. Tail often flicked by male in display.

5. Rounded wings allow the Yellowthroat to flit around in thick vegetation.

4. The Common Yellowthroat has relatively short wings for a migratory bird (some populations don't travel very far).

6. The thin bill is ideal for gleaning insects off foliage.

7. Usually holds onto perch as it grabs insect from leaf, but can also make short flights to snap up flying prey.

8. Throughout North America, thick vegetation close to the ground is the Yellowthroat's prime habitat. Habitats are often wet, such as marshes.

House Wren | *Troglodytes aedon*

Breeds across the northern half of the United States, reaching into Southern Canada in the North, and roughly Central California across to the Carolinas in the south. Winters in the Southeast, Texas, and Mexico.

A FAMILIAR AND NOISY BACKYARD BIRD, found abundantly throughout the North American continent, the House Wren harbors a number of unusual secrets in its behavior. These include a tendency for the male to mate with several females at once, and a very odd habit of destroying the eggs of other birds nesting nearby.

Despite being small and essentially secretive, the House Wren is well known to many, with its small size, cocked-up tail, inquisitive nature, and loud, enthusiastic song. It is a woodland-edge species that has adapted exceptionally well to suburbia, and seems unusually tolerant to the presence of people and their trappings—it is a frequent user of birdhouses.

But the House Wren has a dark side. For reasons that are still unknown, but could include a need for territorial space, this bird frequently enters the nests of other birds (both of the same species and other species), and pricks the eggs, causing them to be infertile. Very few bird species in the world are known to do this.

In the spring, male House Wrens take up territories with one or more nest sites and build one or more "dummy" nests—either constructing a bit of loose nest material, or even a rudimentary cup. When the sexes have paired, the female takes over and completes the nest. If a male has surplus nest sites, he may then pair up with a second female and become bigamous.

10 THINGS TO REMEMBER

1. This House Wren is approaching a Cardinal's nest (House Wrens typically breed in cavities). House Wrens regularly raid other birds' nests and prick the eggs, for reasons unknown.

2. Birds have a long, thin, and downcurved bill used to forage for invertebrates in dense vegetation.

3. Very small in size, as befits a bird that lives low down in dense vegetation.

4. Brown, barred plumage ideal for concealment in undergrowth.

5. Plump body typical of Wrens.

6. Tail is habitually held cocked-up, probably so the bird can advertise its presence to others.

7. [Inset] Commonly crouches like this when threatened by predators.

8. Short, rounded wings for activity in thick vegetation.

9. Bars on tail help to break up the shape of the bird and confuse predators.

10. Pale eyebrow (or "supercilium") is common in many birds and is almost certainly used in communication.

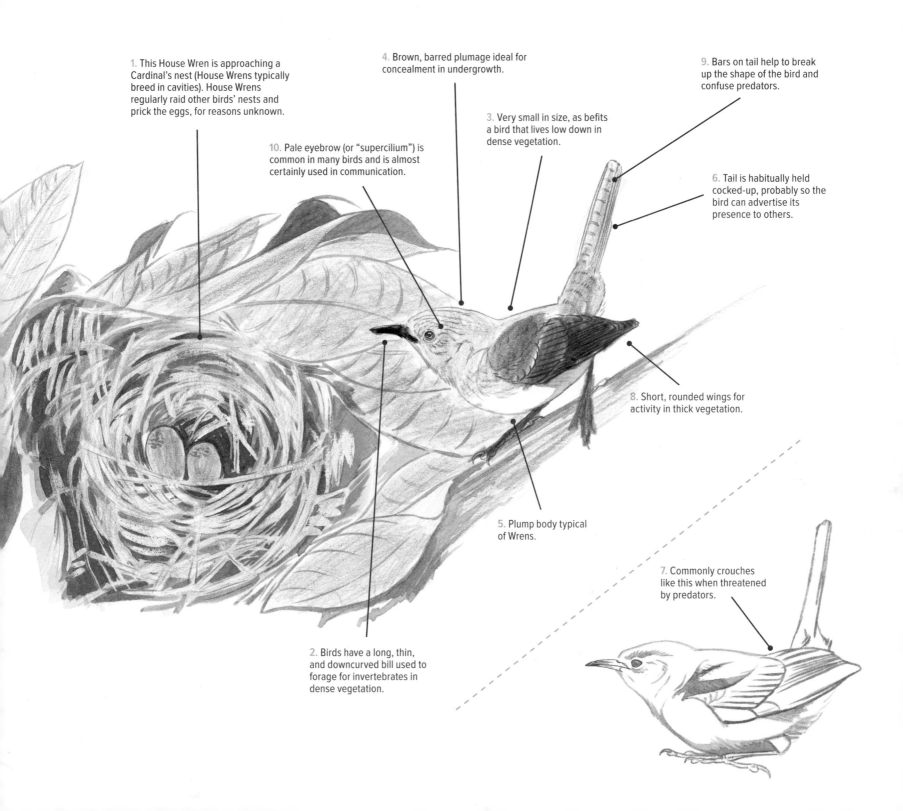

1. This House Wren is approaching a Cardinal's nest (House Wrens typically breed in cavities). House Wrens regularly raid other birds' nests and prick the eggs, for reasons unknown.

10. Pale eyebrow (or "supercilium") is common in many birds and is almost certainly used in communication.

4. Brown, barred plumage ideal for concealment in undergrowth.

3. Very small in size, as befits a bird that lives low down in dense vegetation.

9. Bars on tail help to break up the shape of the bird and confuse predators.

6. Tail is habitually held cocked-up, probably so the bird can advertise its presence to others.

8. Short, rounded wings for activity in thick vegetation.

5. Plump body typical of Wrens.

2. Birds have a long, thin, and downcurved bill used to forage for invertebrates in dense vegetation.

7. Commonly crouches like this when threatened by predators.

Blue Jay | *Cyanocitta cristata*

Found throughout the year in all U.S. states east of the Great Plains, and in much of southern Canada.

Beautiful and intelligent, with an intriguing lifestyle and a few bad habits, the Blue Jay is one of our most recognized birds. It is largely confined to areas east of the Rockies, being replaced in the West by its close relative, the Steller's Jay. The Blue Jay occurs in most well-wooded habitats, and is comfortable in suburbia where it is a frequent visitor to backyard feeding stations.

The Blue Jay is not always popular—on occasion, it will supplement its summer diet by raiding the nests of other birds and eating the eggs or chicks. However, this is very much a peripheral part of its diet, which is largely vegetarian. Most important among plant items are acorns, which the Blue Jay collects and stores assiduously in the fall to use as a supplementary food supply. It is thought that each individual may cache several thousand acorns, hoarded away in hundreds of locations that the bird has to remember.

Blue Jays tend to live in pairs, but at times they will gather together in flocks. These parties have no fixed membership and don't last for very long.

10 THINGS TO REMEMBER

1. Long, stout bill for omnivorous lifestyle.
2. Nasal bristles typical of the crow family.
3. Crest that is raised when the bird is excited or alarmed.
4. Very strong feet.
5. A frequent visitor to bird feeding stations in backyards.
6. Usually feeds at stations on its own, having driven the smaller birds away upon its arrival.
7. Relatively rounded wings are typical for a bird that lives in woodland (for relatively well-controlled, agile flight).
8. Jays and other crows have tough, hard flight and tail feathers.
9. White tips on tail are thought to make birds easier to follow in flock.
10. White throat often shown off in "bobbing" social display, when bird points its head up to the sky.

DID YOU KNOW?

Blue Jays will sometimes clear a feeder of competing birds by imitating the call of a predator, causing competitors to panic and scatter.

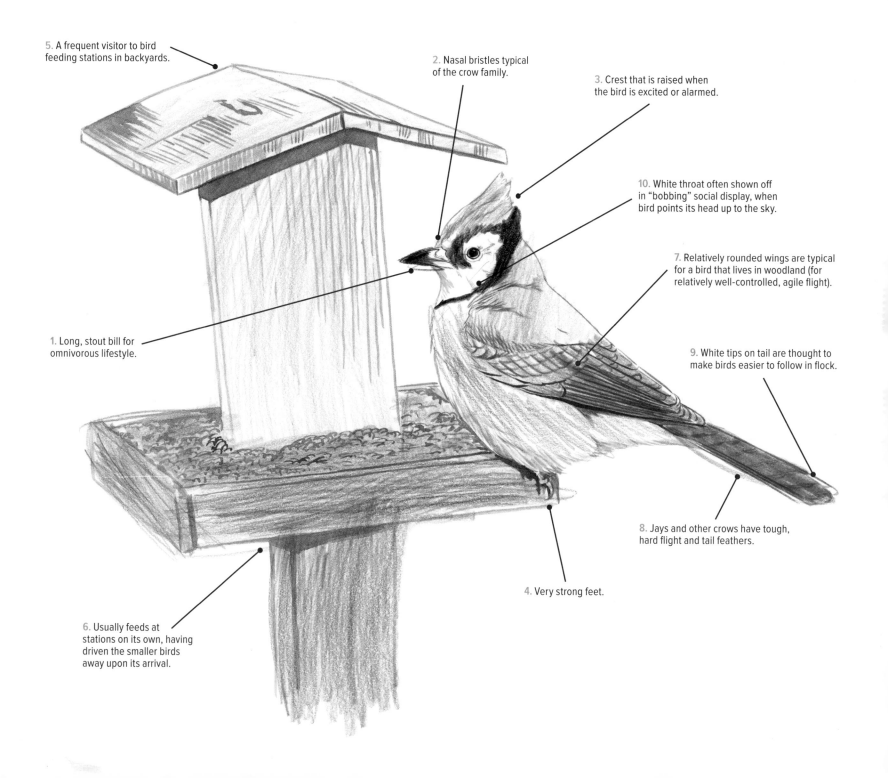

5. A frequent visitor to bird feeding stations in backyards.

2. Nasal bristles typical of the crow family.

3. Crest that is raised when the bird is excited or alarmed.

10. White throat often shown off in "bobbing" social display, when bird points its head up to the sky.

7. Relatively rounded wings are typical for a bird that lives in woodland (for relatively well-controlled, agile flight).

1. Long, stout bill for omnivorous lifestyle.

9. White tips on tail are thought to make birds easier to follow in flock.

8. Jays and other crows have tough, hard flight and tail feathers.

6. Usually feeds at stations on its own, having driven the smaller birds away upon its arrival.

4. Very strong feet.

Black-capped Chickadee | *Poecile atricapillus*

Resident across the northern half of North America, from Alaska across much of Canada below the tree line. Mainly absent south of a line from Oregon in the West to Pennsylvania and New Jersey in the East.

IF THERE IS A CLASSIC EXAMPLE OF A BIRD SPECIES that has benefited from the widespread hobby of feeding birds in the backyard, it has to be the Black-capped Chickadee. Scientists have shown that winter flocks that have feeding stations within their territory have a much better chance of surviving through the winter than those that don't. So although we tend to enjoy the antics of Chickadees as they use their acrobatic skills to take seeds and nuts that we have provided, we are also helping the birds to survive through the winter.

This small bird is still remarkably tough. Many populations live in the cold Boreal forests of southern Canada and Alaska right through the winter. To do this, they have several survival strategies. One is to store excess seeds and even small animals away in caches, which can be retrieved at a later date. Another is to go into a state of torpor (low metabolic rate) at night, reducing their internal body temperature from 108°F (42°C) to 86°F (30°C), thus saving energy.

In the breeding season, Black-capped Chickadees select a natural cavity in a tree for their nest. Both sexes often enlarge the interior through excavation. The female builds a cup nest and may lay 6–8 white eggs with reddish-brown freckles.

10 THINGS TO REMEMBER

1. In winter, the bird has more feathers than in the breeding season, so as to insulate itself against the cold.

2. It is a habitual user of hanging feeders all across the northern half of North America.

3. Usually bustles in to take a single seed and then quickly flies off to store it away for later consumption.

4. Has a short, conical bill.

5. Strong legs and feet enable Chickadee to perform acrobatics such as hanging upside down to reach the underside of branches.

6. Black bib is larger in males than in females.

7. Bold black cap.

8. Very white cheeks help to identify Black-capped from other species of Chickadees.

9. Pale wing panel is usually obvious to the observer and brighter than on other species of chickadees.

10. Fairly long tail is used to help bird balance when it is feeding acrobatically in the branches.

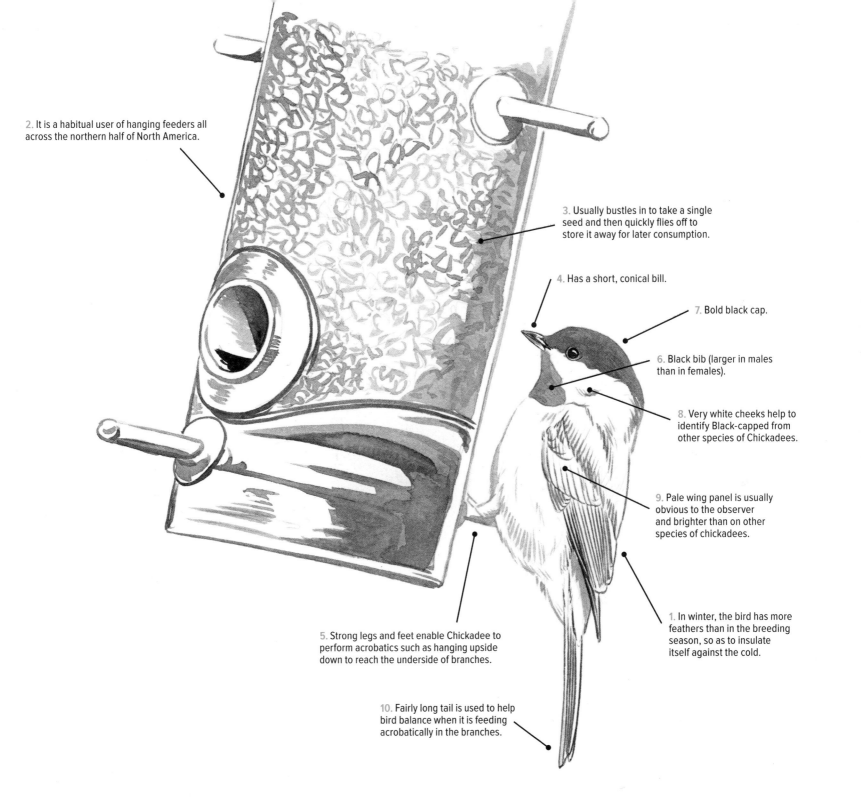

2. It is a habitual user of hanging feeders all across the northern half of North America.

3. Usually bustles in to take a single seed and then quickly flies off to store it away for later consumption.

4. Has a short, conical bill.

7. Bold black cap.

6. Black bib (larger in males than in females).

8. Very white cheeks help to identify Black-capped from other species of Chickadees.

9. Pale wing panel is usually obvious to the observer and brighter than on other species of chickadees.

1. In winter, the bird has more feathers than in the breeding season, so as to insulate itself against the cold.

5. Strong legs and feet enable Chickadee to perform acrobatics such as hanging upside down to reach the underside of branches.

10. Fairly long tail is used to help bird balance when it is feeding acrobatically in the branches.

White-breasted Nuthatch | *Sitta carolinensis*

Occurs throughout the year right across North America, south of a line from British Columbia across to the Great Lakes and Maritime Provinces. Absent from Florida, some of Gulf Coast, Texas, and the Great Plains.

IN MANY WAYS, NUTHATCHES ARE LIKE MINI-WOODPECKERS. They certainly share the same habit of creeping along the vertical surfaces of tree trunks, seeking out invertebrates within the fissures and holes. They also have long, chisel-like bills, and they fly with deep up-and-down undulations. In other ways, however, they are quite different. They don't make their own nest holes and, perhaps most characteristically, they are able to run down (and up) tree-trunks headfirst. Woodpeckers, with their stiff tails and heavy bodies would fall over if they tried to do this. By creeping down tree trunks and branches it is thought that Nuthatches are able to spot food items that are difficult or impossible to see by creeping upward.

The White-breasted Nuthatch is the largest of our four species of Nuthatch, occurring in deciduous and mixed woodland in most of the lower 48 states. Its characteristic "*yank-yank*" call is also a familiar sound in wooded backyards, where it is a habitual visitor to feeding stations. In the fall and winter, it collects seeds and stores them in holes and cracks within its territory, caching them for future consumption.

As might be expected, White-breasted Nuthatches select holes in trees for their nest sites. Fittingly, most holes are those that have been made by their tree-trunk colleagues, the woodpeckers.

10 THINGS TO REMEMBER

1. The bird has a unique habit of running down, as well as up tree limbs. Nuthatches are the only birds that do this.

2. [Inset] Holds on upside down by hanging on with one foot and using the other as a prop.

3. Although body is upside down when hanging, Nuthatches frequently hold their head up to study their surroundings.

4. [Insetl] Very strong feet and long claws enable the Nuthatch to creep up and down branches.

5. Long, chisel-like bill enables the bird to break open hard shells of seeds and nuts by hacking at them.

6. The bill is slightly upturned to peck into crevices.

7. The very short tail is soft, and is of no use in propping up bird (as a woodpecker tail is).

8. Trunks of tree form a stable microhabitat that can provide food year-round.

9. Male has black crown and neck, while female's is blue-gray.

10. Color shade of back varies—palest back color is found in the east of the United States.

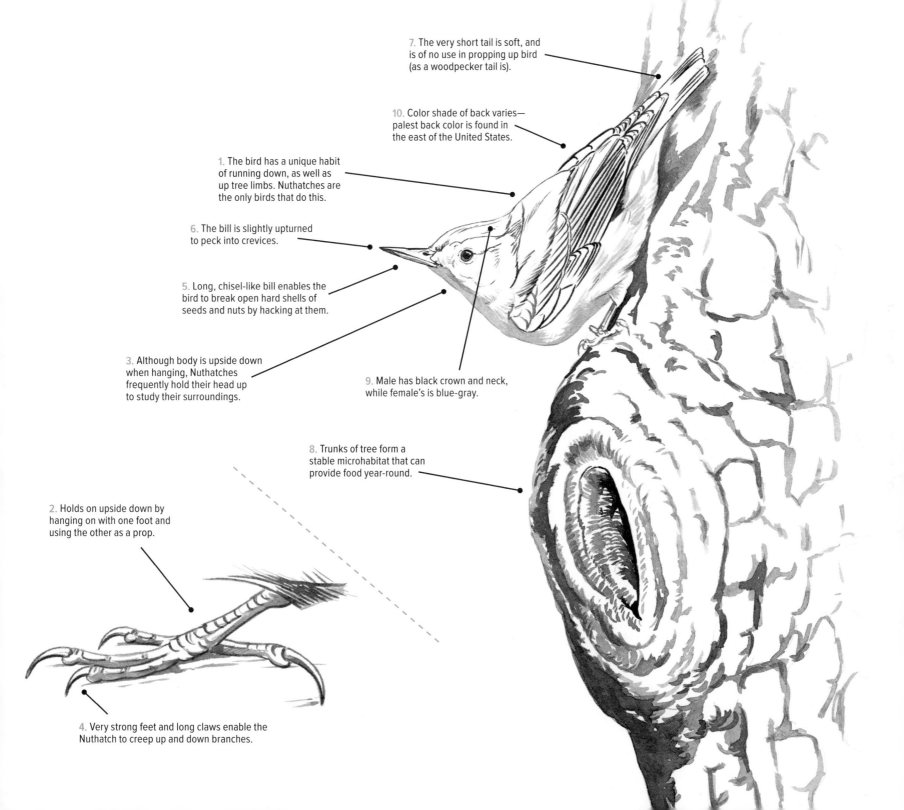

7. The very short tail is soft, and is of no use in propping up bird (as a woodpecker tail is).

10. Color shade of back varies— palest back color is found in the east of the United States.

1. The bird has a unique habit of running down, as well as up tree limbs. Nuthatches are the only birds that do this.

6. The bill is slightly upturned to peck into crevices.

5. Long, chisel-like bill enables the bird to break open hard shells of seeds and nuts by hacking at them.

3. Although body is upside down when hanging, Nuthatches frequently hold their head up to study their surroundings.

9. Male has black crown and neck, while female's is blue-gray.

8. Trunks of tree form a stable microhabitat that can provide food year-round.

2. Holds on upside down by hanging on with one foot and using the other as a prop.

4. Very strong feet and long claws enable the Nuthatch to creep up and down branches.

Eastern Bluebird | *Sialia sialis*

Occurs west of the Great Plains. Present all year from Northern Florida westward to Texas, and then north to Oklahoma, Arkansas, and to Illinois, Ohio, and New York. Mainly a summer visitor north of here, as far as Saskatchewan in the West and Quebec in the East.

THERE ARE FEW MORE POPULAR BIRDS in the whole of the United States than Bluebirds. With their deep-blue coloration, tameness, and readiness to nest in specially provided birdhouses, they ingratiate themselves to householders across the country. In fact, there are three species: Eastern, Western, and Mountain, the latter possessing paler, more powdery-blue coloration than the other two. All three nest in holes and all have distinctly intriguing lifestyles.

It is a shame to shatter a popular bird's reputation, but the idealized impression of the loyal family of backyard Bluebirds is something of a façade. These birds are given to intense aggression, fighting with each other and with other birds over mates and nest sites; not infrequently Bluebirds kill other Bluebirds. Their family relationships can also be complicated. While most are monogamous, some will hold several mates at once (especially Western Bluebirds); even those that have a strong pair bond may still copulate in secret with other members of the opposite sex. Some males actually force copulation on reluctant females.

Bluebirds hunt by watching from an elevated perch and flying down to pounce on ground-living insects. They live in open areas in the summer, but in fall and winter feed on berries and often fly around woodland areas in flocks.

10 THINGS TO REMEMBER

1. Large eyes for spotting prey from a distance of up to 131 feet (40 m).

2. Heavy bill for capturing and killing ground-living insects and other invertebrates.

3. Typically uses high perch and scours open ground for prey.

4. Male is deep blue on upperparts. Individuals vary in the extent of blue color.

5. Male is deep orange on throat and breast.

6. Females are pale versions of the male, but they too vary, with some birds being richer orange on the underparts than others.

7. Nest boxes are regularly used as breeding sites, although the natural site is a hole in a tree.

8. Bluebirds are "socially monogamous." Both have roles within the pair bond and look after the young, but both will readily copulate with other members of the opposite sex.

9. Female is rarely seen far from the nest. She will defend it, sometimes violently, from other females and other birds.

10. In winter, Bluebirds sometimes roost inside nest boxes for warmth.

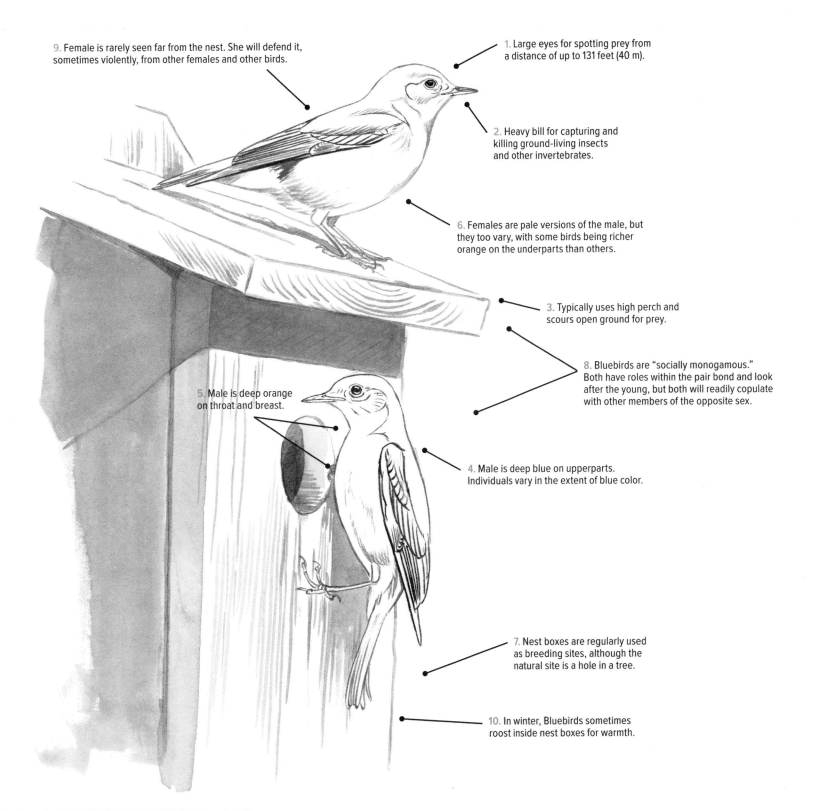

9. Female is rarely seen far from the nest. She will defend it, sometimes violently, from other females and other birds.

1. Large eyes for spotting prey from a distance of up to 131 feet (40 m).

2. Heavy bill for capturing and killing ground-living insects and other invertebrates.

6. Females are pale versions of the male, but they too vary, with some birds being richer orange on the underparts than others.

3. Typically uses high perch and scours open ground for prey.

8. Bluebirds are "socially monogamous." Both have roles within the pair bond and look after the young, but both will readily copulate with other members of the opposite sex.

5. Male is deep orange on throat and breast.

4. Male is deep blue on upperparts. Individuals vary in the extent of blue color.

7. Nest boxes are regularly used as breeding sites, although the natural site is a hole in a tree.

10. In winter, Bluebirds sometimes roost inside nest boxes for warmth.

American Robin | *Turdus migratorius*

Breeds almost throughout the North American continent. Present all year in most of the lower forty-eight states, but primarily a summer visitor to Canada. Common on migration almost anywhere.

POPULAR BIRDS WITH A PLEASANT SONG AND BOLD PLUMAGE, American Robins are a familiar sight in backyards and woodlands right across the country. As the scientific name implies, they are migratory, with northern populations providing a welcome sign of spring when they show in March or April. South of the Great Lakes region, American Robins can be seen at any time of the year.

The illustration opposite gives a typical view of this large member of the thrush family. It can often be seen running across lawns in stop-start fashion, one moment holding its position as it scours the grass for signs of earthworm activity, and then suddenly making a quick sprint and lunge toward whatever it has seen. Besides worms, Robins also eat other insects, which they may glean from the vegetation. In the fall, their diet turns almost exclusively to berries, which they eat in large quantities. At this time of year, they frequently gather into small parties.

The nest of an American Robin is a cup made up from dead grass and twigs, with an inner mud lining and a lining of grass inside that. It can take anywhere from 7–14 days to build, depending on how much mud is available. The female lays 3–4 eggs, and pairs may raise up to three broods a season.

10 THINGS TO REMEMBER

1. Worms are an important food source.
2. Strong, straight bill for dealing with ground-living invertebrates.
3. Long legs allow the Robin to run over grass in stop-start fashion, looking for signs of worms.
4. The ear-openings on a bird are invisible, but are located just behind the eyes. Robins use auditory as well as visual signals to find food in the soil.
5. Grassland is an important feeding ground, although Robins also feed in leaf-litter and take berries from trees.
6. The red breast is what gives the bird its name "Robin," from the common English red-breasted bird.
7. Females have a duller red color on the breast than the male representation in the illustration.
8. Yellow bill with black tip.
9. As far as Robins are concerned, the shorter the grass, the better for foraging. Longer grass conceals prey better.
10. This worm will be a major meal, and may well attract attention from other Robins nearby. This bird will have to be alert to keep its meal.

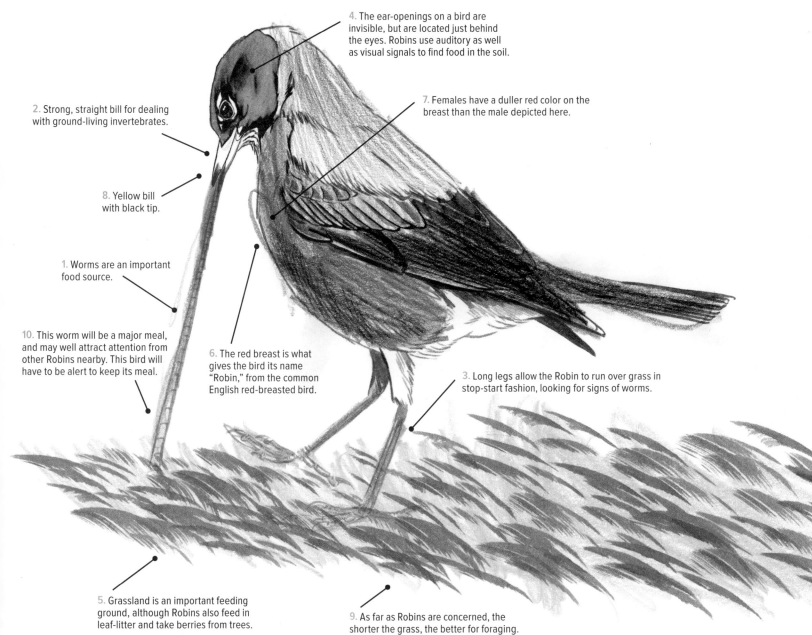

4. The ear-openings on a bird are invisible, but are located just behind the eyes. Robins use auditory as well as visual signals to find food in the soil.

7. Females have a duller red color on the breast than the male depicted here.

2. Strong, straight bill for dealing with ground-living invertebrates.

8. Yellow bill with black tip.

1. Worms are an important food source.

10. This worm will be a major meal, and may well attract attention from other Robins nearby. This bird will have to be alert to keep its meal.

6. The red breast is what gives the bird its name "Robin," from the common English red-breasted bird.

3. Long legs allow the Robin to run over grass in stop-start fashion, looking for signs of worms.

5. Grassland is an important feeding ground, although Robins also feed in leaf-litter and take berries from trees.

9. As far as Robins are concerned, the shorter the grass, the better for foraging. Longer grass conceals prey better.

Northern Mockingbird | *Mimus polyglottos*

Present all year throughout the lower forty-eight states, but only found in the very south of Canada.

ONE OF THE MOST FAMOUS OF ALL SINGERS, perhaps more for the inventiveness and liveliness of its outpourings rather than for their pure musical quality, the Northern Mockingbird provides a soundtrack to much of rural America. In the spring it is indefatigable, singing all through the day and often at night (to unmated males), repeating every phrase a few times before going on to the next. Mockingbirds improve and add to their repertoire as they grow older (they can have up to 200 song types), and every individual male or female has its own special song, which of course includes a large number of imitations of other bird calls. Some of this mimicry is so good that it is hard to separate the real sound from the copy.

As well as being noisy, Northern Mockingbirds are also common, conspicuous, and notably aggressive. In the fall and winter, for example, they will vigorously defend a berry-bearing bush or tree from all other birds, attempting to keep the fruits for themselves. They are also very aggressive in defense of their bulky nest, which tends to be placed low down in a bush.

In the summer Mockingbirds feed mainly on insects and other invertebrates, especially beetles, grasshoppers, and ants. They garner these by running across open patches of ground, including grass, in a stop-start fashion similar to that of an American Robin.

10 THINGS TO REMEMBER

1. Both sexes sing ceaselessly in the spring. If you hear one singing through the night, it is an unmated male.
2. Selects conspicuous perch for singing.
3. White patches on wings are shown off during aggressive displays.
4. White outer tail feathers are also flashed in social encounters.
5. Long legs are typical of a ground-feeding bird.
6. Long tail helps to provide balance on the ground. It tends to be held up as a braking aid when the running bird comes to a stop.
7. Staring yellow eyes.
8. Unspecialized, multi-purpose bill.
9. Pale eyebrow (*supercilium*), seen in many species of birds.
10. Throat can be seen trembling when bird is singing.

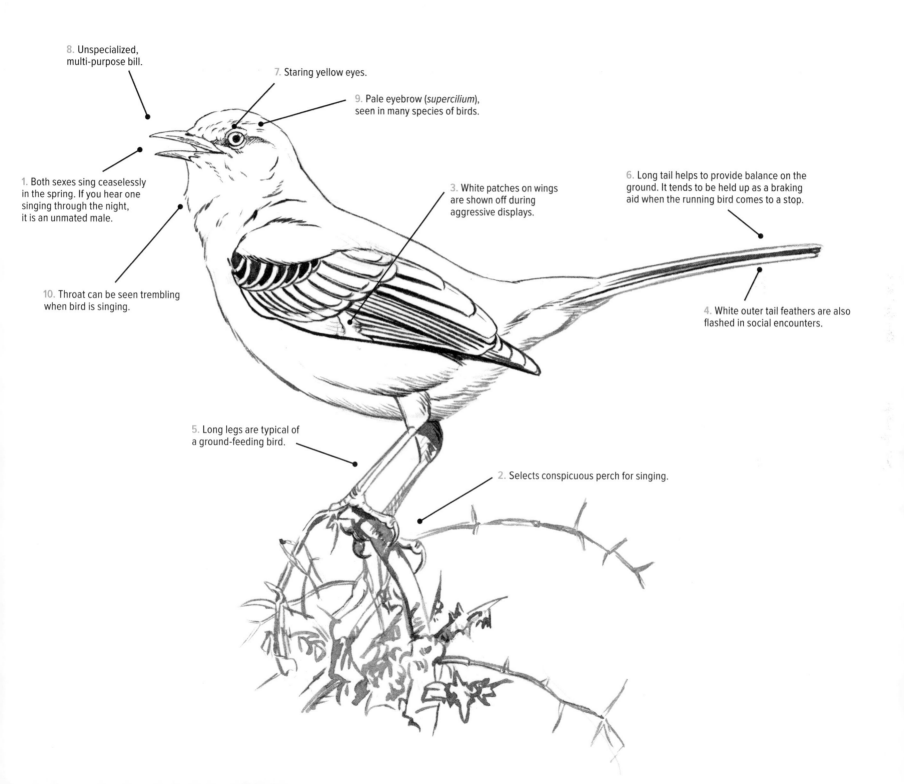

8. Unspecialized, multi-purpose bill.

7. Staring yellow eyes.

9. Pale eyebrow (*supercilium*), seen in many species of birds.

1. Both sexes sing ceaselessly in the spring. If you hear one singing through the night, it is an unmated male.

3. White patches on wings are shown off during aggressive displays.

6. Long tail helps to provide balance on the ground. It tends to be held up as a braking aid when the running bird comes to a stop.

10. Throat can be seen trembling when bird is singing.

4. White outer tail feathers are also flashed in social encounters.

5. Long legs are typical of a ground-feeding bird.

2. Selects conspicuous perch for singing.

European Starling | *Sturnus vulgaris*

Found year-round throughout North America except for Alaska and the northern tundra.

AS ITS NAME IMPLIES, THE EUROPEAN STARLING is not a native of North America. In 1890 and 1891, about 100 birds were released into Central Park in New York, having been brought over from the UK. Allegedly, they found the New World to their liking, multiplied enormously, and now number at least 200 *million* birds, spread over almost the entire continent. It is an astonishing success story, although the birds can be a pest and are not overly popular with humans.

The European Starling is mainly a grassland bird, feeding on the ground, but requiring holes in which to nest. It is extremely sociable, breeding in small colonies and sometimes forming enormous roosts in the winter that can number in the millions. In breeding colonies, the Starling exhibits much skullduggery: both sexes frequently mate with several members of the opposite sex, and females also practice an unusual behavior known as "egg-dumping"—they lay their own eggs in the nests of their neighbors in addition to their own clutch.

Another unusual aspect of the European Starling is its capacity to imitate other birds and sundry environmental sounds. It is not in the class of the Mockingbird, but can still make an effort at such things as alarm clocks, whistles, cell phone ringtones, and even crying babies.

10 THINGS TO REMEMBER

1. Small, starlike whitish spots over the plumage give the Starling its name. There are more spots in the winter, and more on females than males.

2. Spots wear away during winter to give less spotted spring plumage.

3. [Inset] The bill has a bluish-base in males (as illustrated to the right) and is pink in females.

4. Plumage has an oily look and is also iridescent.

5. Strong legs reflect the Starling's main foraging habitat, on the ground and in grassland. It feeds on ground-living invertebrates, including worms.

6. Spiky bill is used for probing into the ground. Bird is able to open the bill once inserted, thus making a hole for seeking prey.

7. [Inset] Forward-facing eyes can rotate forward to give good judgment of distance when bird is looking in a hole.

8. Long wings give characteristic triangular shape in flight.

9. Short tail useful for tight turns in flight.

10. Mainly dark plumage helps to conceal birds on the ground.

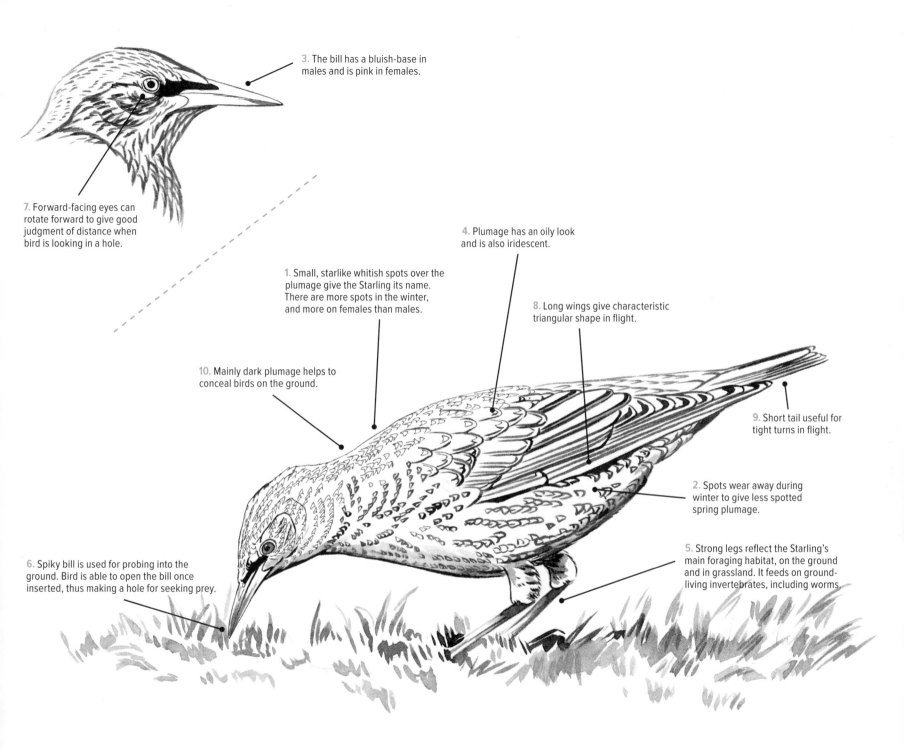

3. The bill has a bluish-base in males and is pink in females.

7. Forward-facing eyes can rotate forward to give good judgment of distance when bird is looking in a hole.

4. Plumage has an oily look and is also iridescent.

1. Small, starlike whitish spots over the plumage give the Starling its name. There are more spots in the winter, and more on females than males.

8. Long wings give characteristic triangular shape in flight.

10. Mainly dark plumage helps to conceal birds on the ground.

9. Short tail useful for tight turns in flight.

2. Spots wear away during winter to give less spotted spring plumage.

6. Spiky bill is used for probing into the ground. Bird is able to open the bill once inserted, thus making a hole for seeking prey.

5. Strong legs reflect the Starling's main foraging habitat, on the ground and in grassland. It feeds on ground-living invertebrates, including worms.

Bohemian Waxwing | *Bombycilla garrulus*

A breeding bird of the northwest, from Alaska to British Columbia, and eastward in Canada to the shores of the Hudson Bay. Outside this region, a winter visitor to the northern Rockies, Great Lakes region, New England, and the Maritime Provinces. Sporadic in appearance.

THERE ARE TWO SPECIES OF WAXWING IN NORTH AMERICA: the familiar Cedar Waxwing, found throughout much of the continent, and the Bohemian Waxwing, mainly confined to the Boreal forests of the West. Both are plump birds with silky plumage which often gather together in flocks.

The life of a Bohemian Waxwing is dominated by its need to find enough of its staple diet—fruit, in the form of berries. It feeds on these for most of the year, even though it will also catch small insects, such as mosquitoes, in short sallying flights, especially during the summer. Nevertheless it is one of the few North American birds that can feed exclusively on fruit without needing anything else. It feeds greedily, and some Waxwings have been known to eat 1,000 berries a day. It swallows them whole, and has an especially broad gape to cope with larger fruits, such as cherries.

The Waxwing is named for the peculiar red extensions to the secondary feathers seen on adult birds. In Bohemian Waxwings, they are indicators of age and sex, with adult males having up to eight extensions, females up to seven, and young birds usually four or five. Birds with more waxy tips tend to have greater reproductive success than those less well adorned.

DID YOU KNOW?

Waxwings will sometimes drink by catching snowflakes in flight.

10 THINGS TO REMEMBER

1. Distinctive crest.
2. Soft, dense plumage.
3. Short, but strong legs allow birds to stretch, or even hang upside down to reach fruits.
4. Usually seen in flocks; very sociable.
5. Never found far from berries, their staple diet.
6. The bill is short and stout, with a small notch which allows the bird to pluck fruits.
7. Gape is unusually wide for the size of the bird, allowing large berries to be swallowed.
8. Peculiar red waxy tips to secondary feathers are indicators of sex, age, and individual quality.
9. Yellow tips to the primary feathers indicate that this is an adult bird.
10. Bold, black face mask.

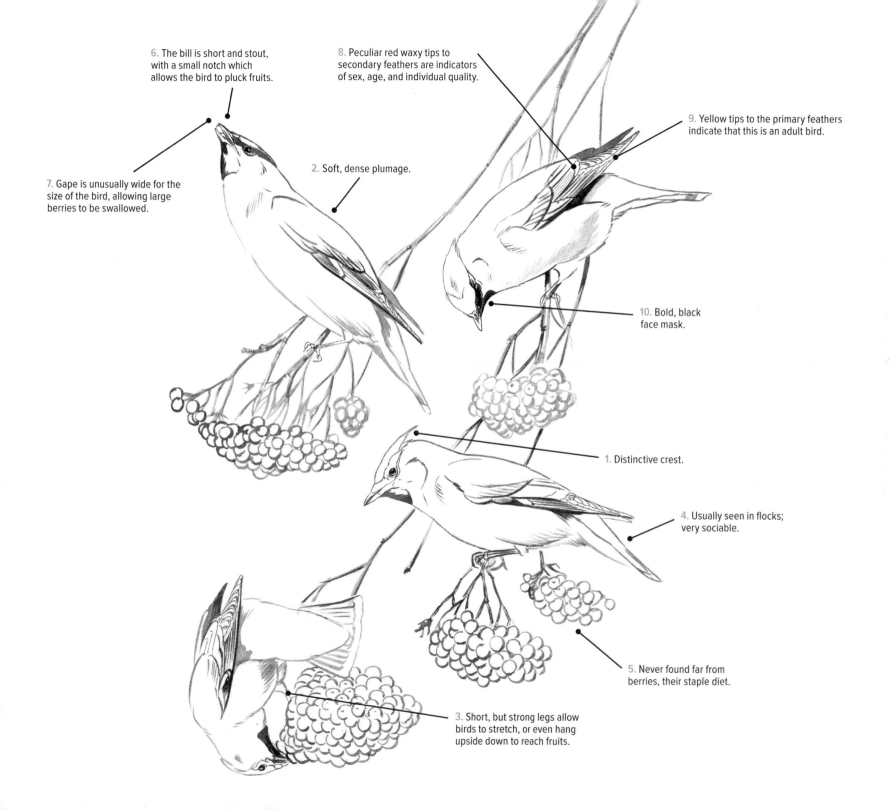

6. The bill is short and stout, with a small notch which allows the bird to pluck fruits.

8. Peculiar red waxy tips to secondary feathers are indicators of sex, age, and individual quality.

9. Yellow tips to the primary feathers indicate that this is an adult bird.

2. Soft, dense plumage.

7. Gape is unusually wide for the size of the bird, allowing large berries to be swallowed.

10. Bold, black face mask.

1. Distinctive crest.

4. Usually seen in flocks; very sociable.

5. Never found far from berries, their staple diet.

3. Short, but strong legs allow birds to stretch, or even hang upside down to reach fruits.

Breeds in the Great Lakes and St. Lawrence forest zones, south to Virginia, Georgia, Alabama, Arkansas, Tennessee, Kentucky, and Missouri. Winters in Central and South America.

ONCE YOU HAVE COLORED IN THE ILLUSTRATION OPPOSITE, you might jump to the conclusion that the male Scarlet Tanager is the sort of bird you couldn't possibly miss. Yet in reality, this denizen of the forest canopy is a shy and retiring bird, keeping to itself, and is remarkably easy to overlook. By the late summer, its exotic plumage has disappeared, and the male Scarlet Tanager becomes a green bird with black wings.

Tanagers usually feed high up in trees, where they pick insects from the surface of leaves and make rapid, fly-catching sallies from a perch. Early in the summer, it concentrates on caterpillars, when these are at their most abundant, but as the weeks pass it turns its attention to beetles, grasshoppers, and crickets. Later still, prior to migration, it begins to eat berries including mulberries, elder, and sumac.

Scarlet Tanagers migrate from the woodlands of eastern North America to the lowland rainforest of the northwestern part of South America. Here it joins large parties of birds of many species that spend their time moving through the forest. Its companions in the winter flock include many other species of Tanagers.

Not surprisingly for a bird of the canopy, the Scarlet Tanager builds its nest fairly high up, usually between 20–33 feet (6–10 m) above the ground. The nest is a shallow cup placed on a horizontal branch.

10 THINGS TO REMEMBER

1. Typically found in the middle and upper canopy of deciduous woods and forests, where it can be difficult to spot.
2. Leaves provide main feeding habitat. In summer, the Tanager picks insects off the surface of leaves.
3. Astonishingly intense red plumage of male. Female is mainly green, with darker wings.
4. In display, male perches below female and lets his wings droop down, accentuating the contrast between red and black on the plumage.
5. Gray bill is a contrast to red head.
6. Stout, pointed bill adapted to eating fruit and large insects.
7. This part of the bird is called the "rump."
8. The tail feathers of a bird are technically called "rectrices."
9. This part of the bird is called the "flanks."
10. This part of the bird is called the "mantle."

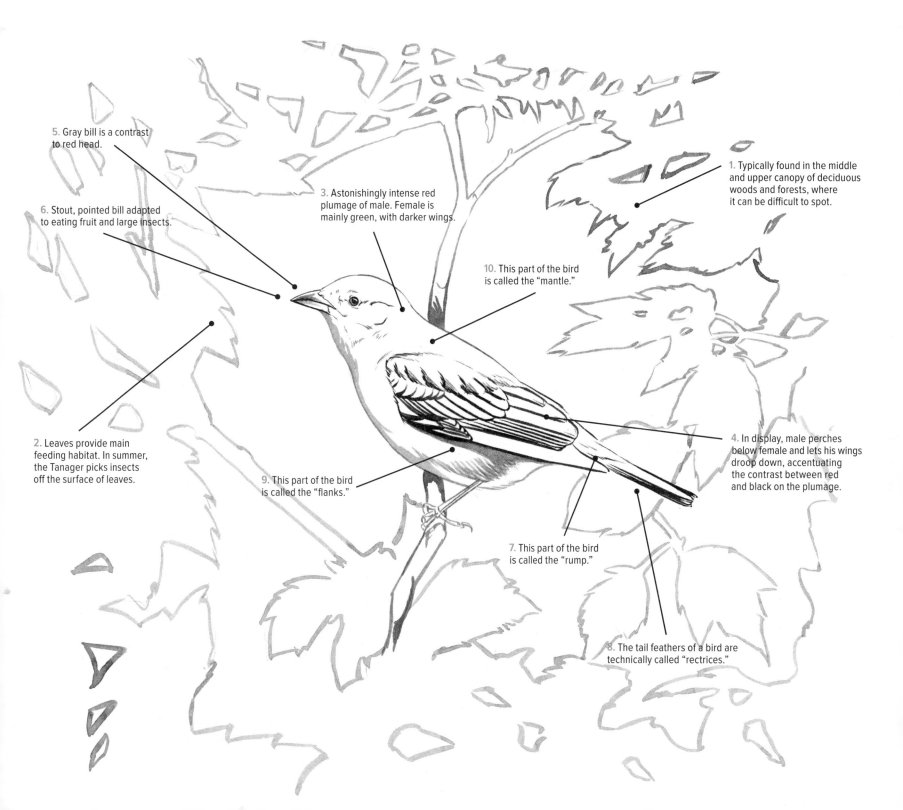

5. Gray bill is a contrast to red head.

6. Stout, pointed bill adapted to eating fruit and large insects.

3. Astonishingly intense red plumage of male. Female is mainly green, with darker wings.

1. Typically found in the middle and upper canopy of deciduous woods and forests, where it can be difficult to spot.

10. This part of the bird is called the "mantle."

2. Leaves provide main feeding habitat. In summer, the Tanager picks insects off the surface of leaves.

4. In display, male perches below female and lets his wings droop down, accentuating the contrast between red and black on the plumage.

9. This part of the bird is called the "flanks."

7. This part of the bird is called the "rump."

8. The tail feathers of a bird are technically called "rectrices."

Northern Cardinal | *Cardinalis cardinalis*

Present all year over the whole of the eastern half of the continent as far north as the Great Lakes. Also creeps in west to New Mexico and Arizona.

THE NORTHERN CARDINAL IS THE SORT OF BIRD that makes people take up the hobby of backyard bird feeding. With its relative tameness, distinctive shape, spectacular plumage (in the male), and gorgeous, musical, whistling song, it is one of the most popular of all species in the eastern half of the continent where it is found. Indeed, it has been voted the official State Bird in seven different states.

Cardinals are attracted to bird feeders simply because they are, at heart, seed-eaters and that's what most people provide. In fact the bill, which is very thick, is designed for opening seeds by crushing them or cutting them open with its sharp sides. A useful tool, the bill is capable of managing almost every kind of seed, together with fruit, flowers, leaf buds, and a wide variety of insects. The Cardinal can even use it to peel grapes and discard the skin.

Both male and female Cardinals sing, but the males sing more and they can be heard almost throughout the year. During the spring they will also sing at night and, given that they vocalize so much, it is just as well that the song sounds extremely pleasing to our ears.

The Cardinal nest is a bulky open cup placed in a thick shrub or vine, not usually very high up. The female lays 3–4 eggs, and both parents feed the nestlings.

DID YOU KNOW?

Sometimes, the female Cardinal sings at the male from the nest to "order" extra effort in finding food for the brood.

10 THINGS TO REMEMBER

1. An indefatigable singer, both by day and sometimes by night in the spring.

2. Bright crimson plumage, which gives the bird its name (after red robes worn by churchmen called cardinals).

3. Female is much dingier, with red mostly on the wings and tail, but also at the tip of the crest.

4. Brightness of red coloration comes from pigments called "carotenoids" found in the Cardinal's diet. The degree of brightness is an indication of mate quality, with the brightest males having the greater reproductive success and the territories with the best cover for nesting.

5. The degree of brightness of red color on the breast is directly correlated to how good the male is at finding food for the young.

6. [Inset] Red bill. Juvenile has black bill, which gradually turns orange. The difference helps birds age each other.

7. [Inset] The tongue helps to position the seed in the bill so it can be cracked open.

8. [Inset] Extremely thick, conical bill which is able to deal with a wide range of seeds, including the very hardest.

9. [Inset] Very large crest. Many social displays show off the crest.

10. Large black patch on throat and around eye.

9. Very large crest. Many social displays show off the crest.

6. Red bill. Juvenile has black bill, which gradually turns orange. The difference helps birds age each other.

8. Extremely thick, conical bill which is able to deal with a wide range of seeds, including the very hardest.

10. Large black patch on throat and around eye.

7. The tongue helps to position the seed in the bill so it can be cracked open.

1. An indefatigable singer, both by day and sometimes by night in the spring.

2. Bright crimson plumage, which gives the bird its name (after red robes worn by churchmen called cardinals).

5. The degree of brightness of red color on the breast is directly correlated to how good the male is at finding food for the young.

3. Female is much dingier, with red mostly on the wings and tail, but also at the tip of the crest.

4. Brightness of red coloration comes from pigments called "carotenoids" found in the Cardinal's diet. The degree of brightness is an indication of mate quality, with the brightest males having the greater reproductive success and the territories with the best cover for nesting.

Painted Bunting | *Passerina ciris*

Found as a summer visitor in two parts of the United States: along the Atlantic Coast from North Carolina to Central Florida, and in the south Mississippi Valley west to Oklahoma, Texas, and New Mexico. Winters in Mexico and south Florida.

THE PAINTED BUNTING IS NOT PARTICULARLY COMMON and is found in a comparatively small part of North America, but it is such a lavish and vividly colored bird that it would be a shame not to include it in a coloring book. So special is the plumage that the young males only begin to show the remarkable combination of blue, green, and red in their second year.

This species is a summer visitor to two distinct regions: the eastern seaboard north to South Carolina, and the Mississippi Valley, including Texas and Oklahoma. In both areas it is a summer visitor, but the eastern birds retreat south to Florida for the winter. Painted Buntings also occasionally wander much further north, where they often delight birders by visiting feeding stations.

This bird is mainly unobtrusive, feeding quietly on the ground for its primary diet of seeds. In spring and early summer, however, it also eats insects and will leave the ground to forage among the leaves of bushes and trees.

One somewhat unexpected feature of the Painted Bunting's behavior is a tendency for males to fight violently in spring. The birds peck at each other's eyes, grapple with their claws, and barge each other. Deaths have been recorded frequently as a result. Access to females is hotly contested, and the very best males often acquire two or more mates.

10 THINGS TO REMEMBER

1. Female plumage is remarkably drab in comparison to well-grown males.

2. Males under one year old also sport this plumage. They only acquire the bright coloration when they're about twelve months old.

3. Pale green plumage is cryptic. The female is responsible for all breeding duties, so needs to keep a low profile.

4. [M] Brilliant red underparts.

5. [M] Vivid blue head. Birds that show such extreme differences in the plumage of males and females are quite often polygamous, and this is also the case for the Painted Bunting.

6. [M] Despite the gaudy coloration, one of the male's main displays is to flutter its wings, which are green and brown!

7. [M] The eyes are often attacked when two males are fighting.

8. Very thick bill allows bird to eat a wide variety of seeds.

9. A fairly common visitor to feeding stations, especially in Florida during the winter.

10. Cutting edge of bill S-shaped, like American sparrows. This helps the bird slice open seeds.

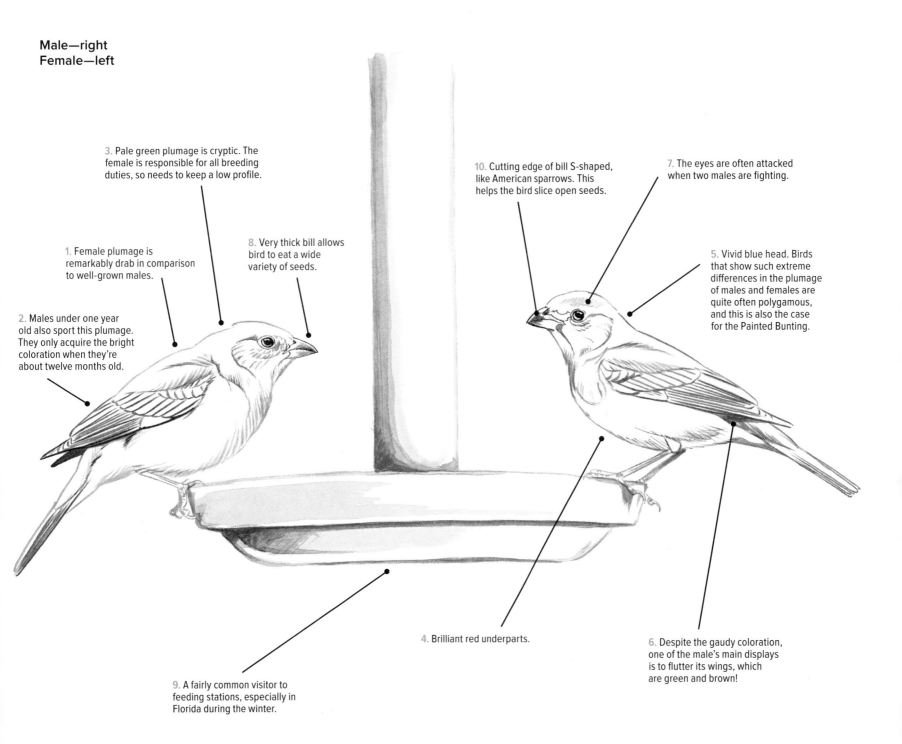

Male—right
Female—left

3. Pale green plumage is cryptic. The female is responsible for all breeding duties, so needs to keep a low profile.

10. Cutting edge of bill S-shaped, like American sparrows. This helps the bird slice open seeds.

7. The eyes are often attacked when two males are fighting.

1. Female plumage is remarkably drab in comparison to well-grown males.

8. Very thick bill allows bird to eat a wide variety of seeds.

5. Vivid blue head. Birds that show such extreme differences in the plumage of males and females are quite often polygamous, and this is also the case for the Painted Bunting.

2. Males under one year old also sport this plumage. They only acquire the bright coloration when they're about twelve months old.

4. Brilliant red underparts.

6. Despite the gaudy coloration, one of the male's main displays is to flutter its wings, which are green and brown!

9. A fairly common visitor to feeding stations, especially in Florida during the winter.

A breeding bird of the taiga forest belt, from Newfoundland and Labrador west to Nunavut and the Northwest Territories, south to Alberta and east to the Great Lakes. Winters along the Pacific coast, and over much of eastern North America.

COLOR IS EXTREMELY IMPORTANT FOR THE WHITE-THROATED SPARROW—in particular the color of the wide stripe over the eye. There are two forms of White-throated Sparrows, those with white stripes above the eye and those with tan-colored stripes above the eye. These differences occur in both sexes and, remarkably, they are reflected in the individual behavior of the bird. Males with white stripes sing more frequently than tan-striped birds, they are generally more aggressive, and they are more likely to stray outside the pair bond to copulate with other members of the opposite sex. On the other hand, tan-striped birds of both sexes are better parents, being more assiduous in bringing good food supplies to the young.

When it comes to mating, a white-striped bird almost always mates with a tan-striped bird, which is why both forms survive. That's because the dominant white-striped females prefer the homely tan-striped males, leaving the rest to mate with each other.

The White-throated Sparrow is a common woodland bird that resides north of the Great Lakes, where its delightful "Old Sam Peabody" song is a dominant component of the Boreal forest soundscape. In common with other sparrows, it feeds mainly on insects in the summer, switching to seeds for the duration of the fall and winter. It is a frequent visitor to feeding stations, usually in small groups.

10 THINGS TO REMEMBER

1. Sings the distinctive, slow, tuneful "Old Sam Peabody" song in spring from a prominent perch.

2. The brown coloring and stripes typical of a small, ground-feeding species help to camouflage the bird while it's feeding.

3. Strong legs. Has an unusual method of scratching for food on the ground, using 1–4 rapid kicking movements of both legs. Can forage in deeper litter than other sparrows.

4. [Inset] Sparrow bills have an S-shaped edge to lower mandible that helps them cut seeds open.

5. Distinctive white throat separates them from other sparrows.

6. Yellow patch between eye and bill. This part of the face is known as "the lores."

7. Stripes over the eye are mainly white in this bird. As a white-striped bird, it will be more aggressive and promiscuous than the bird in the inset illustration.

8. [Inset] The stripes over the eye are pale brown (tan). This bird will be less aggressive and a better provider of food for its young than the bird in the main picture.

9. Stripe on top of head varies in the same way as eyebrow (supercilium).

10. [Inset] Black stripe through eye can also be flecked with brown on this tan-striped individual.

7. Stripes over the eye are mainly white in this bird. As a white-striped bird, it will be more aggressive and promiscuous than the bird in the inset illustration.

9. Stripe on top of head varies in the same way as eyebrow (supercilium).

6. Yellow patch between eye and bill. This part of the face is known as "the lores."

2. The brown coloring and stripes typical of a small, ground-feeding species help to camouflage the bird while it's feeding.

1. Sings the distinctive, slow, tuneful "Old Sam Peabody" song in spring from a prominent perch.

5. Distinctive white throat separates them from other sparrows.

3. Strong legs. Has an unusual method of scratching for food on the ground, using 1–4 rapid kicking movements of both legs. Can forage in deeper litter than other sparrows.

8. The stripes over the eye are pale brown (tan). This bird will be less aggressive and a better provider of food for its young than the bird in the main picture.

10. Black stripe through eye can also be flecked with brown on this tan-striped individual.

4. Sparrow bills have an S-shaped edge to lower mandible that helps them cut seeds open.

Red Crossbill | *Loxia curvirostra*

Present all year in the taiga forest belt and mountain coniferous forests. Found in a band from Newfoundland west to Quebec, Ontario, the Great Lakes, and southern Canada to Alberta, British Columbia, and southern Alaska. Also in the Rockies and northwest Pacific coast forests.

ONE OF NORTH AMERICA'S MOST HIGHLY SPECIALIZED BIRDS, the Red Crossbill is found in the conifer woods and forests of the taiga (forest belt south of the tundra) and in the mountains. It lives in flocks that roam forests in search of cones that are ripening, and once it has found them, it will breed and continue to breed until the food supply runs out. It is essentially nomadic, moving in a random direction after breeding rather than following any set migratory patterns.

The Crossbill's extraordinary bill is adapted to open the scales of conifer cones. The bird applies the tip of its lower mandible to the side of the scale, and the act of shutting the bill causes the scale to be forced back, releasing the seed. Experiments have shown that these birds cannot feed efficiently without the crossing.

Amazingly, the bills of some birds cross to the left and others to the right, just as humans are left- or right-handed. Left-twisted birds approach the cone from the left-hand side and, if the cone is detached, hold it in their left foot. Young Crossbills, on the other hand, don't have crossed bills until they are 27 days old, and only when they are 45 days old can they feed effectively.

For breeding, the main variable is food supply, rather than season, although these birds cannot breed in late fall. They frequently begin breeding through the cold months of December and January, and birds have been found incubating eggs even when the outside temperature is as low as -2°F (-19°C).

10 THINGS TO REMEMBER

1. Confined to coniferous woodland and forest. Also occurs in hemlock and fir stands.

2. Requires the presence of cones that are ripening and opening for feeding.

3. Large, heavy-headed finch with strong neck muscles.

4. Male has unusual brick-red color, females are green, and juveniles streaked brown.

5. Short, forked tail.

6. Strong legs and feet allow Crossbill to hold onto cones and twigs, even upside down. Often uses both legs and bill (clenched onto twig) to clamber around, in a similar manner to a parrot.

7. Some individuals are left-footed and others right-footed: it depends on the way the mandibles cross.

8. [Inset] Exceptionally unusual bill. Lower mandible crosses underneath upper mandible. This is almost unique among birds.

9. [Inset] Lower mandible may cross to right of upper mandible (as in illustration) or to left. It depends upon the individual.

10. Thick plumage to insulate from the cold.

8. Exceptionally unusual bill. Lower mandible crosses underneath upper mandible. This is almost unique among birds.

3. Large, heavy-headed finch with strong neck muscles.

4. Male has unusual brick-red color, females are green, and juveniles streaked brown.

9. Lower mandible may cross to right of upper mandible or to left. It depends upon the individual.

10. Thick plumage to insulate from the cold.

6. Strong legs and feet allow Crossbill to hold onto cones and twigs, even upside down. Often uses both legs and bill (clenched onto twig) to clamber around, in a similar manner to a parrot.

7. Some individuals are left-footed and others right-footed: it depends on the way the mandibles cross.

5. Short, forked tail.

1. Confined to coniferous woodland and forest. Also occurs in hemlock and fir stands.

2. Requires the presence of cones that are ripening and opening for feeding.

American Goldfinch | *Carduelis tristis*

Found throughout temperate North America at some time of year, mainly as a summer visitor in the North and a winter visitor in the South.

ONE OF THE SUBURBAN UNITED STATES' MOST POPULAR BIRDS, the effervescent American Goldfinch is a common visitor to backyard feeding stations, where it delights householders with its colorful plumage and pleasing antics. It is extremely sociable, rarely being found alone and instead gathering in small and occasionally large (300+) flocks. Within smaller, more stable flocks there is a hierarchy—certain individual males and females are dominant over their colleagues, taking first pick of good food sources.

These birds are strongly associated with thistles and other related plants, and spend a great deal of time feeding upon them. They prefer to forage on standing plants, and can often be seen clinging onto swaying stems, flapping their wings to keep balance. Their bills are long and thin, adapted to prying into the bracts and opening them up to reveal the seeds inside.

Goldfinches have a very late breeding season, beginning well after most other songbirds have finished, in July and August. This could well be related to the fact that they feed their young almost exclusively on seeds (not insects), and the main thistle crop is in late summer. They build remarkable nests out of plant stems and roots, lined with thistle down, which are so compact that they are reputed to be able to hold water.

10 THINGS TO REMEMBER

1. Sociable—almost always found in flocks, even during the breeding season.

2. Birds keep individual distance when feeding.

3. Males are bright yellow. Some are more brightly colored than others, which probably reflects their state of health.

4. Black crowns are shown off in aggressive head-forward display.

5. Females are less yellow and have a plain head.

6. Birds are specialist feeders on thistles and related plants.

7. Goldfinches are acrobatic, often feeding upside down and using strong feet to hold on to slender stems and bracts.

8. Narrow bill for reaching in-between the bracts of seed-heads.

9. [Inset] To feed, Goldfinch inserts bill in-between bracts and then opens bill, releasing the seeds. Possesses extremely strong muscles for opening and closing the bill.

10. The bright orange bill color comes from pigments called "carotenoids," which are found in their diet. The brighter the bill, the more attractive the bearer to the opposite sex.

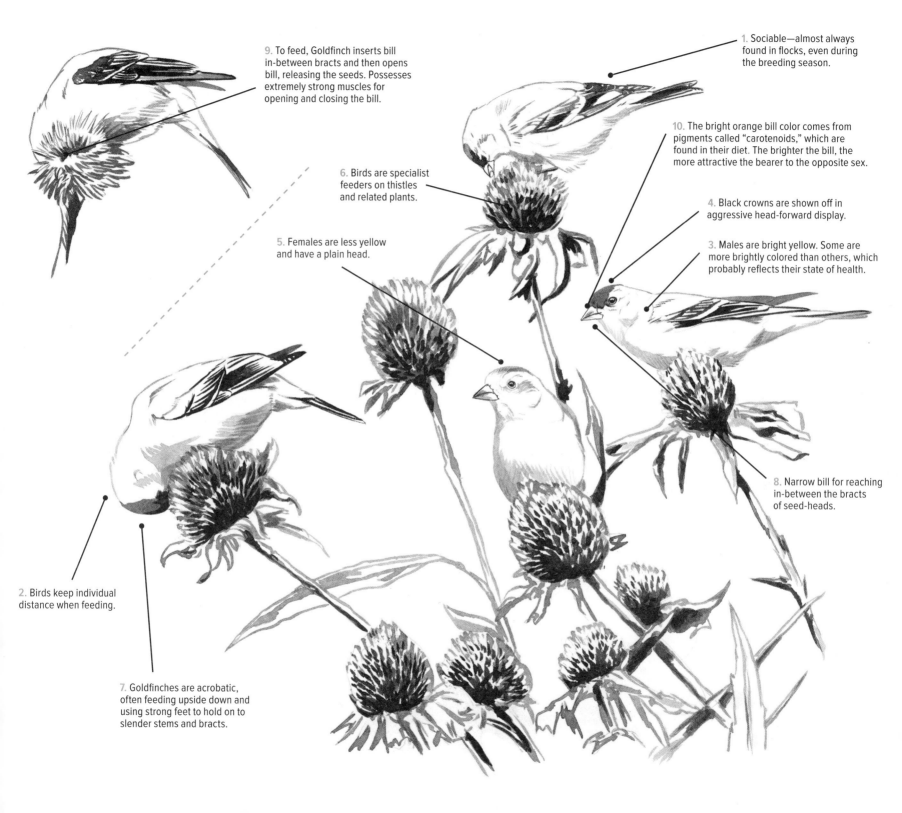

9. To feed, Goldfinch inserts bill in-between bracts and then opens bill, releasing the seeds. Possesses extremely strong muscles for opening and closing the bill.

1. Sociable—almost always found in flocks, even during the breeding season.

10. The bright orange bill color comes from pigments called "carotenoids," which are found in their diet. The brighter the bill, the more attractive the bearer to the opposite sex.

6. Birds are specialist feeders on thistles and related plants.

4. Black crowns are shown off in aggressive head-forward display.

5. Females are less yellow and have a plain head.

3. Males are bright yellow. Some are more brightly colored than others, which probably reflects their state of health.

8. Narrow bill for reaching in-between the bracts of seed-heads.

2. Birds keep individual distance when feeding.

7. Goldfinches are acrobatic, often feeding upside down and using strong feet to hold on to slender stems and bracts.

Eastern Meadowlark | *Sturnella magna*

Present all year throughout eastern North America as far north as the Great Lakes. A summer visitor to much of New England, Quebec, Michigan, and Minnesota. Also occurs in the deserts of Arizona, New Mexico, and Texas.

IF YOU SPOT A FLASH OF YELLOW IN THE UNDERGROWTH, it is more than likely a Meadowlark as it is flushed from the roadside or alights on a nearby fencepost. This is one of the most common and most iconic grassland and farmland birds, beloved by many for its sweet, if slightly melancholy song. It occurs primarily on the eastern side of the country, being replaced in the west, appropriately enough, by the Western Meadowlark. In the zone of overlap where the two species meet, the Eastern Meadowlark tends to be found in fields with taller, lusher grass. Yet strangely, in the Southwest, a race of the Eastern Meadowlark occurs instead in desert grassland.

In common with many birds of any habitat, the Eastern Meadowlark feeds mainly on insects in the summer and seeds in the fall and winter. It acquires all of these by foraging on the ground, and is able to dig for food with its long, very sharp bill. Its favorite summer foods are grasshoppers and crickets, along with some beetles and caterpillars.

In the spring, the male defends its territory using song, both on the ground and in flight. Ground and flight songs are slightly different. Once the birds have paired up, the male makes quite a complicated nest on the ground, shaped like a dome with a fitted roof. It is not at all uncommon for male Meadowlarks to be polygamous; indeed, about 50–60 percent of the population will have more than one mate at any one time. Some birds have three.

10 THINGS TO REMEMBER

1. The bill is long with a sharp tip. Meadowlarks have an unusual feeding method called "gaping," which involves inserting the bill into the soil and then opening it to make a hole. The jaws have very strong muscles to open the bill.

2. Upper mandible (or "culmen") is flattened so that the bill fits easily into the earth.

3. Frequently sings in flight.

4. Spreads tail in display flight.

5. White outer tail feathers are conspicuous and may act as a signal to other birds.

6. When flying, wings are beaten very quickly, making the bird resemble a Quail or other game bird.

7. Large, conspicuous black crescent on breast.

8. The edge of the cheeks (ear-coverts) are white. This is one of the few distinctions from the Western Meadowlark, which has yellow ear coverts.

9. Upperparts yellowish and streaked, rendering feeding birds very inconspicuous.

10. Yellow breast is often puffed out in display.

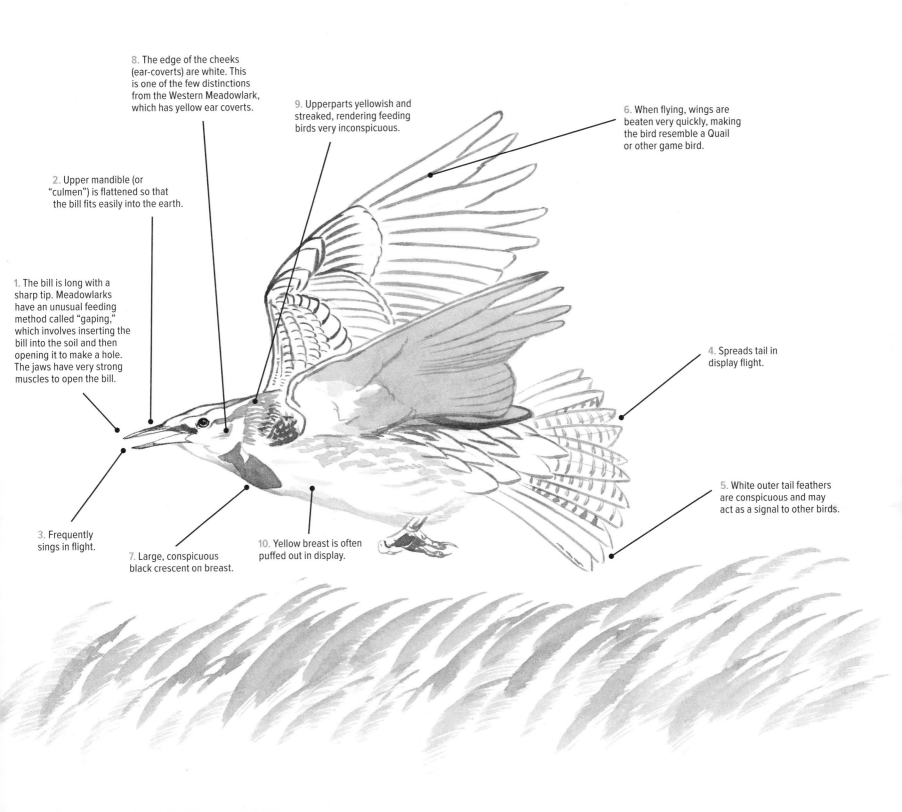

8. The edge of the cheeks (ear-coverts) are white. This is one of the few distinctions from the Western Meadowlark, which has yellow ear coverts.

9. Upperparts yellowish and streaked, rendering feeding birds very inconspicuous.

6. When flying, wings are beaten very quickly, making the bird resemble a Quail or other game bird.

2. Upper mandible (or "culmen") is flattened so that the bill fits easily into the earth.

1. The bill is long with a sharp tip. Meadowlarks have an unusual feeding method called "gaping," which involves inserting the bill into the soil and then opening it to make a hole. The jaws have very strong muscles to open the bill.

4. Spreads tail in display flight.

3. Frequently sings in flight.

5. White outer tail feathers are conspicuous and may act as a signal to other birds.

7. Large, conspicuous black crescent on breast.

10. Yellow breast is often puffed out in display.

Common Grackle | *Quiscalus quiscula*

Mainly a bird of the east, where it is a resident from Florida to New England and from Texas to Oklahoma and the Dakotas. North and west of here it is a summer visitor, as far west as New Mexico and as far north as Alberta.

NOT THE MOST POPULAR OF OUR BIRDS, the Common Grackle is nonetheless a beneficiary of human actions. The clearing of forests in the last couple of centuries has greatly expanded the area of open landscapes where the bird thrives, and the practice of building shelterbelts in prairie regions over the last 50 years has also helped it to expand west.

The Common Grackle is a member of the American Blackbird family (*Icteridae*), with its dark plumage, spiky, probing bill, and tendency to walk rather than hop over the ground when foraging. It is an omnivore, eating all kinds of foods including insects, earthworms, fish, small rodents, grain, berries, and seeds. It will also, unfortunately, predate the eggs and young of other birds, and has even been known to kill and eat adult songbirds.

In common with other Blackbirds, the Common Grackle is highly sociable. It will often breed in small colonies, and in the fall and winter it frequently gathers in large feeding and roosting concentrations. The latter can be formidable, containing up to 1 million birds, sometimes including Blackbirds, Cowbirds, and Starlings, too. The roosts are usually in stands of conifer trees and often next to a wetland area. They can be so large and noisy, and the birds can deposit so much feces, that they are considered a health hazard and a nuisance by locals.

Conifers are the usual nesting site for females. They build a bulky cup-shaped nest deep inside the trees' branches. Evergreens are suitable because Common Grackles are among the first U.S. birds to nest in the springtime, with eggs already laid in the nest by March.

10 THINGS TO REMEMBER

1. Very sociable. Usually seen in flocks or small parties.

2. Feeds on the ground, walking across open areas.

3. The bill is short, but pointed, and the bird is able to "gape" like a Meadowlark to forage insects from the soil.

4. Yellow eyes are very distinctive.

5. Glossy, iridescent, bronzy feathers on the body and wings.

6. Females aren't as glossy as males, especially on their back.

7. Inside the bill is a keel on the palate, which helps the bird to pierce hard seeds.

8. [Inset] Wedge-shaped tail has outer feathers above inner ones, producing a "keel." Males have a display in which they lower inner feathers to exaggerate the "V."

9. [Inset] Slight keel shape of long tail helps to prevent stalling when bird lands and banks during flight. In level flight and when flying into the wind, the tail is kept flat.

10. Bill-up display, with head raised is often given as a warning signal to intruders.

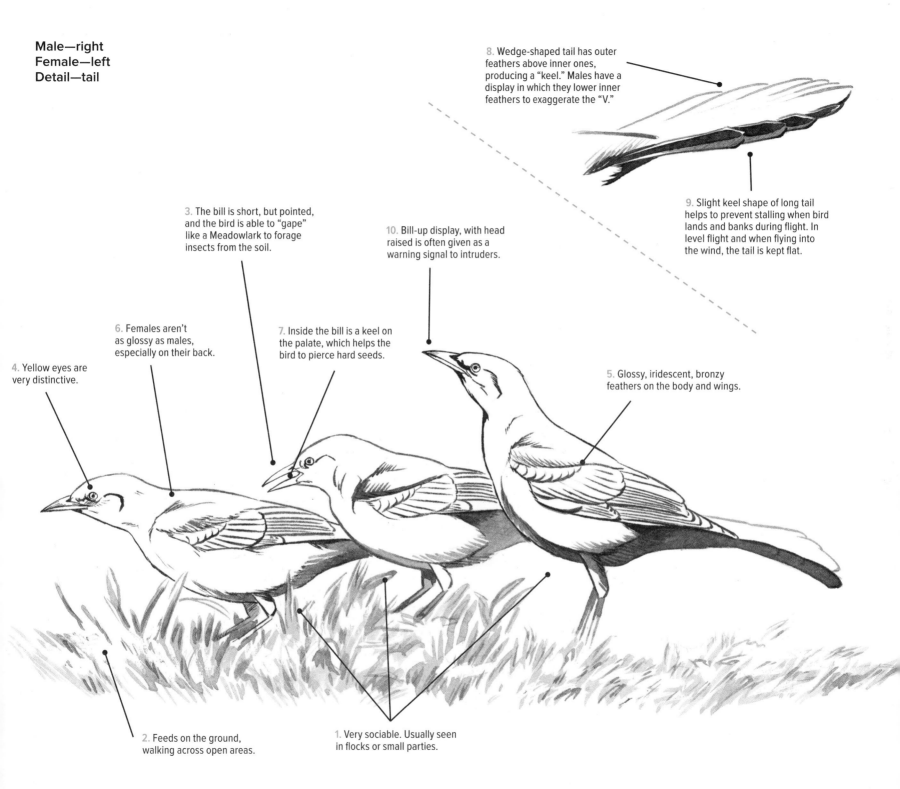

Male—right
Female—left
Detail—tail

8. Wedge-shaped tail has outer feathers above inner ones, producing a "keel." Males have a display in which they lower inner feathers to exaggerate the "V."

9. Slight keel shape of long tail helps to prevent stalling when bird lands and banks during flight. In level flight and when flying into the wind, the tail is kept flat.

3. The bill is short, but pointed, and the bird is able to "gape" like a Meadowlark to forage insects from the soil.

10. Bill-up display, with head raised is often given as a warning signal to intruders.

6. Females aren't as glossy as males, especially on their back.

7. Inside the bill is a keel on the palate, which helps the bird to pierce hard seeds.

5. Glossy, iridescent, bronzy feathers on the body and wings.

4. Yellow eyes are very distinctive.

2. Feeds on the ground, walking across open areas.

1. Very sociable. Usually seen in flocks or small parties.

Red-winged Blackbird | *Agelaius phoeniceus*

Breeds throughout North America except Alaska and the extreme north. In Canada, the Great Lakes region, and New England, it is mainly a summer visitor; otherwise present all year.

IF YOU EVER WONDERED WHAT THE MOST ABUNDANT BIRD IN NORTH AMERICA IS, the answer is probably the Red-winged Blackbird. Population estimates are difficult to make, but it is thought that there could be 190 million individuals in the United States during the winter. They occur pretty much everywhere from coast to coast, but their primary habitat is large freshwater marshes. They also prefer fields, croplands, and even upland meadows.

The Red-winged Blackbird is also one of the world's best studied species, and perhaps the most striking findings about its life are concerned with pairing up. This species is highly polygamous, with males frequently pairing up with several females; incredibly, the record is of one male with 15 mates. The females have no qualms about sharing their mate, and it benefits them to breed close to other females in their mate's territory, because together the females can defend their nests more effectively. Many females will also enter the territory of another male and copulate with him if they are so inclined.

Almost everybody knows the male Blackbird's bizarre song—a few introductory notes leading to an explosive gurgling buzz. This song is customarily delivered with wings slightly open, exposing their brilliant red epaulets.

Outside of the breeding season, Red-winged Blackbirds often roost in very large numbers, sometimes in millions, along with Grackles, and other sociable birds. The roosts often form in major grain-producing farming areas, where the birds are considered a pest. Some individual birds have been recorded flying 50 miles (80 km) to join a nighttime roost, although the average is only 9 miles (14 km).

10 THINGS TO REMEMBER

1. Most typical breeding habitat is marshes, especially cattails.
2. The bird sings from the top of cattails.
3. When singing, the bird spreads its wings and raises its red epaulets.
4. Epaulets are the main territorial flag. In experiments carried out by scientists, males with blackened epaulets tended to lose their territory. Males intruding in a territory usually cover theirs up.
5. Epaulets also have a yellow outer edge.
6. The bird spreads tail in display.
7. In late summer, the epaulet border may fade to white.
8. Has black plumage typical of its relatives, but lacks any gloss.
9. Strong, long legs for walking on the ground. It is able to hop backward and scratch at the same time, which is unusual.
10. The bill is typical of the family, long and sharp. It is able to "gape" like a Meadowlark or Grackle.

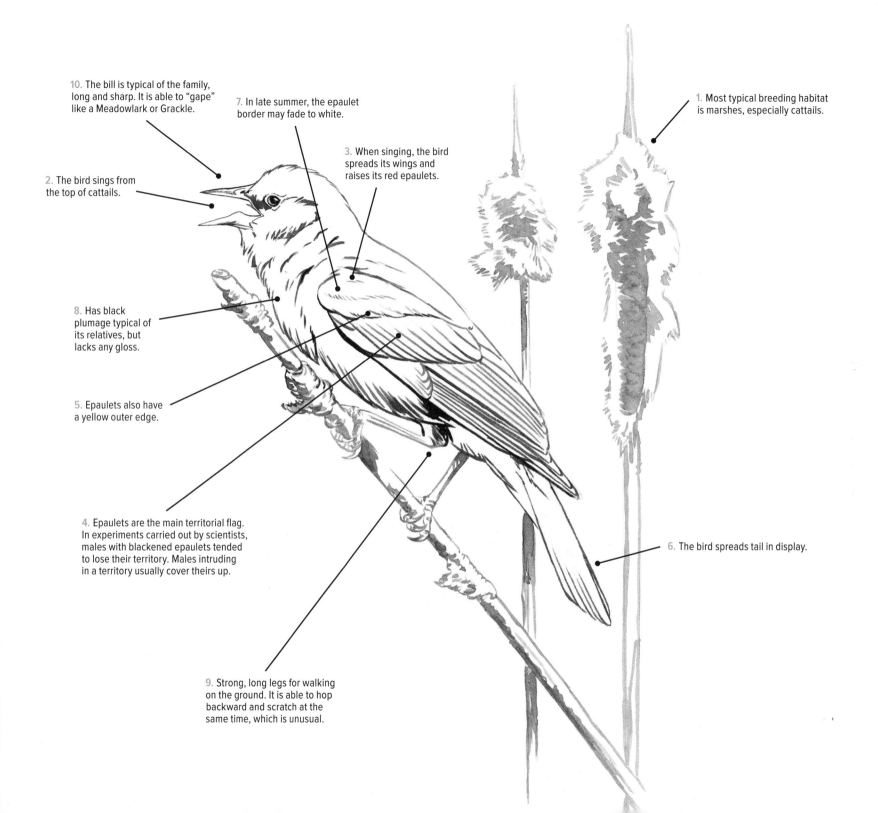

10. The bill is typical of the family, long and sharp. It is able to "gape" like a Meadowlark or Grackle.

7. In late summer, the epaulet border may fade to white.

1. Most typical breeding habitat is marshes, especially cattails.

3. When singing, the bird spreads its wings and raises its red epaulets.

2. The bird sings from the top of cattails.

8. Has black plumage typical of its relatives, but lacks any gloss.

5. Epaulets also have a yellow outer edge.

4. Epaulets are the main territorial flag. In experiments carried out by scientists, males with blackened epaulets tended to lose their territory. Males intruding in a territory usually cover theirs up.

6. The bird spreads tail in display.

9. Strong, long legs for walking on the ground. It is able to hop backward and scratch at the same time, which is unusual.

BIRDS IN FULL COLOR

Western Grebe

Brown Pelican

Northern Pintail

Long-tailed Duck

Tufted Puffin

Magnificent Frigatebird

Ivory Gull

Black Skimmer

Reddish Egret

American Flamingo

California Condor

Sharp-shinned Hawk

Peregrine Falcon

Rock Ptarmigan

Greater Sage Grouse

Northern Jacana

American Golden Plover

American Avocet

Bar-tailed Godwit

Ruddy Turnstone

Wilson's Phalarope

Eastern Screech Owl

Common Poorwill

Greater Roadrunner

Ruby-throated Hummingbird

Belted Kingfisher

Acorn Woodpecker

Northern Flicker

Western Kingbird

Red-eyed Vireo

Violet-green Swallow

Golden-crowned Kinglet

Cape May Warbler

Common Yellowthroat

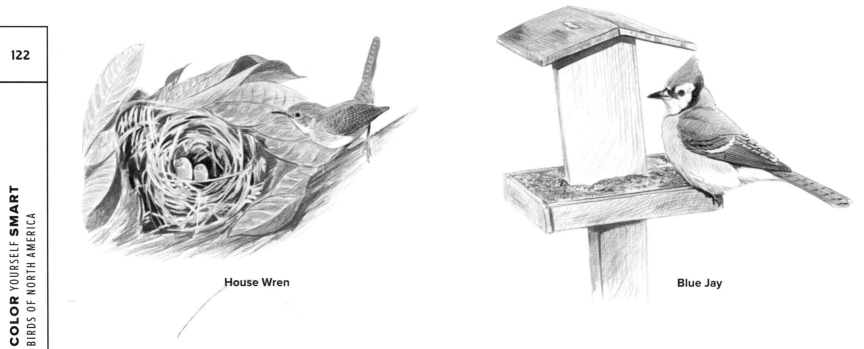

House Wren

Blue Jay

Black-capped Chickadee

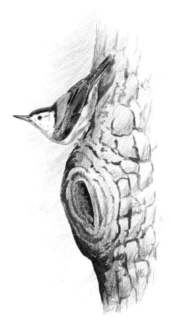

White-breasted Nuthatch

Eastern Bluebird

American Robin

European Starling

Northern Mockingbird

Bohemian Waxwing

Scarlet Tanager

Northern Cardinal

Painted Bunting

White-throated Sparrow

Red Crossbill

125

COLOR YOURSELF **SMART**
BIRDS OF NORTH AMERICA

American Goldfinch

Eastern Meadowlark

Common Grackle

Red-winged Blackbird

QUIZ

1. Which bird is the world's fastest moving animal?

2. What is the main feeding method of the American Avocet known as?

3. What is unusual about the breeding behavior of the Acorn Woodpecker?

4. Which duck dives deeper than any other?

5. What is the unusual and not fully explained behavior that sheds a sinister light on the House Wren?

6. How many female partners can a male Red-winged Blackbird have, if it is very fortunate?

7. Which North American bird is able to imitate the calls of predators so that it can make competitors flee from a feeding station?

8. What common North American bird sings a song rendered "Old Sam Peabody"?

9. What part of the body is almost completely lacking in Grebes?

10. How many berries can a Bohemian Waxwing consume in the course of a single day?

11. Which rare North American bird always feeds with its head upside down?

12. Which common North American bird creeps down trees head first?

13. How does the Eastern Bluebird catch most of its food?

14. Which is the only bird in the world, found in North American deserts, that can effectively hibernate by remaining in torpor for days on end?

15. How does the California Condor kill its prey?

16. Which bird of the High Arctic seems to have an irresistible attraction to red objects?

17. Which shorebird with a broad diet has been known to eat soap?

18. How long does the tongue of the Northern Flicker stick out beyond the tip of the bill?

19. How does the Black-capped Chickadee survive on cold winter nights in the North?

20. Where does a Common Grackle usually put its nest?

21. What is the very specific favorite food of the Cape May Warbler during the breeding season?

22. What are the visible "ears" of the Eastern Screech Owl actually used for?

23. Which small backyard visitor builds its nest so well that it is supposed to be able to hold water?

24. What is unusual about the bones of a Frigatebird?

25. When the American Golden Plover is feeding, does it use its sense of vision most, or its sense of touch?

26. How far can a Northern Pintail reach down when it is "up-ending"?

27. What remarkable record is currently held by the Alaskan population of the Bar-tailed Godwit?

28. In how many states is the Northern Cardinal the official State Bird?

29. How does the male Golden-crowned Kinglet differ from the female?

30. What is the main food of the Sharp-shinned Hawk?

31. How do Greater Roadrunners warm themselves up on a cold morning in the desert?

32. Where does the Violet-green Swallow nest?

33. What is unusual about the feet and toes of the Rock Ptarmigan?

34. On what sort of water would you expect to find a Brown Pelican living and breeding?

35. What aspect of a Red-eyed Vireo's behavior readily distinguishes it from that of a warbler?

36. What is strange about the breeding arrangements of the Wilson's Phalarope?

37. How fast does the Ruby-throated Hummingbird beat its wings when hovering?

38. How many song types can a Northern Mockingbird sing?

39. What color is a Northern Jacana's frontal shield?

40. Do European Starlings have more whitish spots on their plumage in the summer or in the winter?

41. What is the favorite food of the Red Crossbill?

42. At what time of day does a Western Kingbird habitually sing?

43. How does a Black Skimmer feed its young?

44. How high up does the Scarlet Tanager usually put its nest?

45. Why do Common Yellowthroats have such loud voices?

46. How many fish has a Tufted Puffin been known to carry in its bill at any one time?

47. Which North American bird will sometimes spread its wings to make shade in water to trick and attract fish?

48. What is the term for a displaying gathering of the Greater Sage Grouse (and other species)?

49. How long can the nesting burrow of a Belted Kingfisher be?

50. How long does it take for a young, male Painted Bunting to acquire its gaudy coloration?

51. What sort of nest does an Eastern Meadowlark make?

52. What is the American Robin's favorite fall food?

QUIZ ANSWERS

1. Peregrine Falcon

2. Scything

3. It is cooperative. Several males and females live in a group and contribute to feeding the nestlings.

4. Long-tailed Duck

5. It raids the nests of other birds and pricks the eggs

6. 15

7. Blue Jay

8. White-throated Sparrow

9. The tail

10. 1,000

11. American Flamingo

12. (White-breasted) Nuthatch

13. It spots it from an elevated perch and swoops down to grab it with the bill.

14. Common Poorwill

15. It doesn't. It is a scavenger, feeding on animals that are already dead.

16. Ivory Gull

17. Ruddy Turnstone

18. 1.6 inches (4 cm)

19. It lowers its body temperature to cut down heat loss.

20. In a conifer

21. Spruce Budworm

22. Expressing emotion

23. American Goldfinch

24. They are the lightest of any bird of comparable size.

25. Vision

26. 19.7 inches (50 cm)

27. Longest continuous flight by a non-seabird 6,400 miles (10,300 km)

28. 7

29. It has an orange patch on the crown.

30. Birds

31. They allow the sun to heat the skin on their back by ruffling the feathers.

32. A hole in a tree

33. They are feathered

34. Salt water—the sea

35. Slow and sluggish instead of quick and feverish

36. The roles of the sexes are reversed, so that the male builds the nest, incubates the eggs, and tends the chicks alone.

37. 80 times a second

38. 200

39. Yellow

40. The winter

41. Conifer seeds, especially spruce

42. Dawn (or first light)

43. By regurgitation

44. 19–33 feet (6-10 m).

45. They need loud voices to express themselves in thick vegetation, since they don't easily see one another.

46. 29

47. Reddish Egret

48. A lek

49. 6.5 feet (2 m)

50. One year—in its first fall

51. A domed one

52. Berries